Looking Through the Sea of Glass

Four Inspirational Words from God

Ardith Arnelle` Price

AJAP Heavens Edge
Ardith Arnelle` Price
CHRISTIAN
AUTHOR

Contents

Preface   vii

1. Purification   1
   Sea of Glass

   A Day of Darkness and Gloom   11

   The Blood and Water   25

2. Salvation   35
   War-Weary Christians – The Coming Prophecy

   Stages of Life   47

   God's Body is Outside of the City   53

3. Repentance   57
   Fire in Man!

   Fire on the Mountain   63

   The Blue Flame and the Rainbow   69

   Is Not My Word like a Fire?   79

4. Belief   85
   Yeshua is the WORD

   Mold Me and Mend Me   97

   Harmony with God   103

   Hallelujah! I Made it!   111

   Summary   117

   Books By Author   119

   About the Author   123

   Appendix   125

   Bibliography   127

   References   129

   Notes   131

Printed by CreateSpace, An Amazon.com Company

Second Edition: March 2018

Printed in the United States of America

ISBN-10:1985176084 (eBook)

ISBN-13:9798726525808 (pbk.)

Information about external hyperlinks in this book ebook.

Please note the footnotes in this ebook may contain hyperlinks to external websites as part of the bibliographic citations. These hyperlinks have not been activated by the publisher, who cannot verify the accuracy of these links beyond the date of publication.

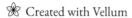 Created with Vellum

Rev 15:2, TLV, "And I saw something like a sea of glass mixed with fire, and those who had overcome the beast and his imagte and the number of his name standing by the sea of glass, holding the harps of God."

Preface

This book will focus on four topics that will prepare; believing Christians, luke-warm Christians, and unrighteous people for the return of Yeshua Messiah (Jesus the Messiah) after false peace have been proclaimed upon the earth.

The year 2018 in Hebrew Bible numerology means harmony and completeness; this symbolic hidden code is called a gematria in the Hebrew language. This number also means judgment for the nations. This coming together under God for unification for all nations must be established, before the coming of Yeshua Messiah. He must authenticate a comprehensive modification in the world, so that the nations, which war with each other, will come together in peace; especially those nations against Israel. A complete transformation must be intrinsically enacted from the old spirit of wickedness to a new spirit of godliness. The destruction of nations will be swift and complete for those nations that reject the covenant with Yeshua Messiah according to His laws and statutes.

The word *chaos* is a Hebrew word (tohu -תֹהוּ) describing the condition of the earth; confusion which is a mass of nothingness, sculpted into a spiral ball that, God created to become a time in our universe, which comes from His spoken Word. This intricate pattern is Elohim Adonai's (God Almighty) secret; mankind will not discover the full measure of the mystery until he has become an immortal Spirit with God in eternity. All that has been written in the Scriptures are true and breathed from Adonai. We are living in chaos today because; we were warned in the writing of the Prophets and the Apostles that these terrible days would be upon us. Now that we are living the "days of terror", the Scriptures are being fulfilled in front of our eyes; we now must address our plight and know that our time on earth is only a whisper away.

This book has been a labor of love. The purpose of this book is to prepare all Saints of God and unrighteous people on earth to get ready for the journey to eternity. This is the last move of the Ruach (Holy Spirit) that has been breathing, on mankind to connect with the Heavenly Father. If there is no connection to God and repentance of our sins, then Elohim Adonai will not allow mankind to enter into His presence. Messiah Yeshua spoke about His coming when He was on earth, many people could not accept the message of "Good News", and mankind continued doing evil without a thought of repentance. We as the modern man are performing the same evilness and vileness in the face of Holy God; if we don't change quickly then, we are doomed for Hell and the pit of eternal fire away from the face of Holy God.

The Holy Spirit has revealed so much to me during this journey of seeking and asking constantly for more wisdom and understanding. El Shaddai (Almighty God) has granted me my request, so this book has been the answer from my only true love and that is Almighty Holy God. My quest to move closer to El Shaddai has led me to embark on studying and learning Hebrew during the 2017 year. Fulfillment and authority in Jesus Christ finally reside inside my Spirit, in ways unknown to the average man who has not found salvation. Salvation is more than just stating that you are a Christian. Salvation is the culmination of three sources, your <u>Body</u>, <u>Soul</u>, and <u>Spirit</u> they all must be in harmony. When they share harmony then, they are like a complete song where the melody is melodious and perfect.

I found studying Hebrew from a Jewish Israeli teacher, during the 2017 year was the culmination of finding "truth" that had been hidden from all Christians for thousands of years. You cannot learn the scriptures without tapping into Hebrew, Greek, and Latin languages. I already knew Latin and had studied some Greek, but Hebrew was a new language to be explored and absorbed into my being. I had sung Hebrew as a singer, but only phonetically.

I secured a chance to really study conversational and historical Hebrew ramifications; that was established in scripture, instantly my Spirit just opened up to new pinnacles of knowledge. I became an acquaintance of a Messianic Rabbi in New Zealand. He inspired and taught me valuable Historical Jewish culture, through his blogs and email writings that I never knew existed.

My knowledge of the Hebrew language has grown exponentially, so when I read and study Scriptures now; I want more actualities and cannot wait to grasp more comprehension of the Hebrew language. Therefore, I have used many Hebrew words and phrases throughout this book. I have provided a terminology page for the many Hebraic words used within the book, as well as, the use of the names of God in many occurrences.

I pray that the book "Sea of Glass" will establish a yearning in your heart, to learn and study the Holy Scriptures and be a "fired-up" Christian for Messiah Yeshua; so when He calls you to make a change in your life, you will be ready. We will follow the path of <u>Purification</u>, <u>Salvation</u>, <u>Repentance</u>, and <u>Belief</u> in Almighty God, and how it impacts lives of all people. Everyone must have a relationship with Almighty God before they can enter into Heaven. I am so honored to be Messiah Yeshua's mouthpiece, during this critical time in history to bring the Word, in these 'Last Days" on this earth.

Ardith Arnelle`Price
Blessed Saint of God Almighty and earthly Gate Keeper for Yeshua HaMashiach (Jesus, the Messiah) "Pray for the peace of Jerusalem"
Sha'alu Shelom Yerushalâyim (Hebrew)
Ps 122:6

***

Read the next book and leave review: *Just The Edge of God; The Touch of His Garment is All We Know*
Thanks again for your support!
Website: https://drmozart18.com/

"Thank you for reading the book. If you enjoyed this book or found it useful in search of knowing Yeshua/Jesus, I'd be very grateful if you'd post a short review on Amazon. Your support does make a difference, and I read all the reviews personally so I can get your feedback and make this book even better."

Note to Readers:
Many Hebrew terms are used though-out the book. These words identify the person of God for the Gentile reader. The rationale for the Hebraic words is to let the Gentile person know they have a Jewish Father in Heaven. Therefore, Christians worldwide must be equipped to embrace Hebraic roots to understand End-Time prophecy.

To my wonderful husband who always supports all of my efforts. To my peace-loving friend Gloria who gave me inspiration from the moment we met who now lives with the Angels. She always said "Love God and have faith" with her sweet calm spirit. - September 10, 2017...

"In the twinkling of an eye" 1 Corinthians 15:52

Chapter 1

Purification

Sea of Glass

"AND I SAW WHAT LOOKED LIKE A SEA OF GLASS glowing with fire and, standing beside the sea, those who had been victorious over the beast and its image and over the number of its name. They held harps given them by God." (Revelation 15:2, NIV)

Water represents the purification of the body and soul. It becomes a symbol for the outpouring of God's Holy Spirit and blessing. We seek the purified water for the thirsty individual who wants to know Yeshua, not as the mortal God-Man who died on the cross; but as the true Messiah Yeshua, who died as our advocate for all mankind. Yeshua is the only one who could have died for our sins. He desired a mortal man to have descendants that would worship and honor Him as the Creator of the Universe. God wanted to experience our pain of sin in our mortal bodies; Yeshua stepped forth and became the proportion of sin, yet did not sin, to obtain an accurate picture of our suffering in sin.

Isaiah 44:3 speaks of the "Living water" that continually moves in the earth and will be poured out on the offspring of mankind who accept God's blessings. By the baptism into the water of the earth, these bodies must be purified by God, as

Yeshua was baptized by His cousin John the Baptist. The stagnant water found in a pond, river, or spring cannot cleanse a lackluster Soul. Your soul must be vibrant and ready to receive the Word of God, without conditions and misconceptions. We must be transported and cleansed by God, ready to receive the gift of eternal life, which accepts an everlasting, immortal Soul.

The Scripture in Revelation 15:2 speaks of a literal "sea of glass" that has "fire" yet crystal clear, and Saints with harps in their hands singing, to Almighty God for His goodness and praising His Holy name; because they believed in Messiah Yeshua (Messiah Jesus) until death and into eternity? How can anyone read this scripture and not get goosebumps and feel the fire of God and His awesomeness? How beautiful this scripture reveals God's love and passion for humankind. He wants all men to come and live with Him. This is why, He created the earth so that we could live with Him and experience the beauty that He so painstakingly created, nurtured, and breathed His breath into all creation to partake and enjoy.

There is another side to Elohim Adonai (Almighty God). He is not a man like we are, and trying to fool Him can lead to death quickly. This happened to Ananias and Sapphira in (Acts 5:11, NIV) "Great fear seized the whole church and all who heard about these events" they kept back monies destined for the Christian cause, and then they lied about their sin. God is everywhere with eyes watching your every move 24/7, never sleeping. In Proverb 15:3 (NIV), "The eyes of the LORD are in every place, Watching the evil and the good." Therefore, we cannot escape Almighty God's hand, and we must be extremely careful how we perform our daily tasks because the Holy Spirit is actively taking notes.

Let's look at how we can get to the "sea of glass" in Heaven - what will be the steps you have to take to secure your Heavenly home?

What is the "sea of glass"? The scripture says in Revelation 4:6

(NIV), "Also in front of the throne, there was what looked like a sea of glass, clear as crystal." Imagine the throne of the "Most High God", who is sitting in the Heavens with His Son Messiah Yeshua on His right-side, high and lifted up as in the Isaiah 6:1? The Prophet Isaiah encounters, for the first time, Messiah Yeshua. Believe it or not, every time there has been an encounter with God, whereby man has encountered Jesus (Yeshua), the spirit and soul of man have to be purified. Before man sinned in the Garden of Eden - Jesus (Yeshua) was always our Father because the Triune God knew the man would fall and Yeshua would become our lamb sacrifice. I know there will be theological arguments on - what Isaiah saw and rebuttal about Old Testament Prophets; however, the Bible speaks of Jesus Christ throughout the sacred Scriptures.

Purification is a step mankind has to take to come before the throne of Almighty God. Messiah Yeshua came so that we do not have to give a blood sacrifice on an altar - as our Jewish cousins performed ages ago because Yeshua is our sacrifice. We must truly be repentant in our soul and spirit before we can enter Heaven. Hebrews 9 explains how we are to worship before the throne of Almighty God through the blood sacrifice of Yeshua and what it really means to become a purified Christian or Messianic Jew.

Yeshua died once for all and took on every vile sin that could ever happen on this earth. Take a moment and think about that statement; it should bring tears to your eyes. We are in a spiritual war on this earth. This is the fire that was shown mixed with the water in the "sea of glass" in Heaven. Our fire is the trials and testing we must endure before we are purified.

Becoming a Christian is not a passport into Heaven. It is more than stating, "I am a Christian" and going through the motions, and saying all of the correct words and prayers. You can say and do all the right things and still not be a true believing Christian. The heart can be changed, but the flesh is still the same, and you have not changed your vile habits. Yet, most Christians believe this is all they have to do in order to enter into Heaven. Just say and do all the correct Christian-ease lingo, and they will enter Heaven. WRONG! You will be left behind.

What is Christian-ease lingo anyway? The Christian-ease lingo is words that people have been saying for years, such as "Amen", "Praise the Lord". All of these words are nothing in the sight of Almighty God because if the heart of the man has not changed, scripture says - they are vain words in the sight of Almighty God (Eph 5:6). There has to be a transformation from the inside of you to the outside, and the spirit and the soul have to be in agreement. If your inner being has not changed, you stand before Almighty God in disobedience and be judged for unrighteousness.

Those saints standing before Holy God had given their lives in opposition to Satan, who proceeds to give them an ultimatum either worship him or die. They choose death rather than take the mark of the beast and bow before the antichrist. This is the true image of godly saints who truly believe in the Holy God. This is the image we should be portraying every day. We should have a mindset set on godly things, thereby leaving worldly lusts behind. If someone tells you that all of the other religions are equal to Christianity, they are wrong. There is only one GOD, and He is Elohim ADONAI – in Exodus 20:3, (NIV) "You shall have no other gods before me."

Also, in Isaiah 44:6, (NIV), "Thus says the Lord, the King of Israel and his Redeemer, the Lord of hosts: I AM THE FIRST and I AM THE LAST; besides me, there is no god."

These verses clearly state who we should worship, and as a matter of fact, we should not mention other gods on our lips. Exodus 23:13, (NIV) "Pay attention to all that I have said to you, and make no mention of the names of other gods, nor let it be heard on your lips."

If you hear anyone who is pastoring to you mention other

gods, and think it is satisfactory to speak as if you can mix all other gods with Elohim ADONAI, "run away from that person or place" as fast as you can. If you stay, you will be subject to antichrist principals and will miss Heaven. You will be in direct disobedience to God and His judgment on you. Stay alert at all times; this is why you have to pray, repent of sins daily and have a REAL relationship with Messiah Yeshua, and then you will be completely transformed and ready to meet your Holy Father. Remember: only God knows your heart, and HE is watching you. Even though you might look good on the outside to everyone else, you might be evil on the inside because the change never took place in your soul and spirit.

There is a date on the Jewish calendar that causes one to pause and contemplate the meaning of life. Elul 25 documents the date of creation of the world and six days later Rosh Hashana – the Jewish New Year which commemorates the birth of mankind. Elul happens to be the twelfth month of the civil year and the sixth month of the religious year. The month of Elul can appear in the months of September or late October, depending on how the moon phases occur around the earth.

The "sea of glass" and the creation of the world (Elul 25) share something exceptional. A prototype of the Garden of Eden is present in Heaven, complete with the Tree of Life and a river with the Water of Life. This model represents the purification of the righteous Saints for eternity that came under Adam's sinful nature, our forefather. This finalizes the process from mortal man (how we live today in our sinful bodies) to immortal man (pure and righteous spiritual bodies) purified and sanctified before Holy and Righteous Messiah Yeshua. This transformation of our spiritual nature finalizes complete forgiveness from Almighty God against all generations from the Beginning of Creation to the End of Time.

The month of Elul is the last month of the Jewish year; Elul is a time of introspection and self-examination in preparation for the coming New Year. It is customary to blow a Shofar after morning prayers (except Shabbat) to remind the Jewish people of the approaching days of judgment known as Rosh Hashanah and Yom Kippur. Messianic Jews and Christians celebrate the major holidays of the Jewish calendar. If you attend a Messianic Congregation, you will celebrate Jewish and Christian holidays, and you will find your understanding of the Scriptures to be complete and humbling. In the scripture of Revelation 22:1 (TLV), an angel shows Apostle John events that will happen in the future. "Then the angel showed me a river of the water of life-bright as crystal, flowing from the throne of God and of the Lamb."

The Saints that came through the Tribulation were purified by fire when they were on earth because they refused to get the "Mark of the Beast" but chose to worship Jesus Christ and believe God's Word. Rosh Hashanah should remind Gentiles of the coming judgment and the "Gathering of the Saints" to Messiah Yeshua. An observation for all Gentiles - should be to repent daily, not just on Rosh Hashanah since Gentiles are not Jewish – there should be a reverence of Yeshua regardless of the High Holy days celebrated by our Jewish cousins even if you attend a Messianic Congregation. There should be repentance daily, asking for forgiveness to those you have maltreated in any way, thereby completing the salvation circle to become the transformed person of God, which all Gentiles and Messianic Jews aim to acquire.

The beginning of the world was spoken into existence by God the Father with the Son who is Messiah Yeshua by His side. Elul 25 is the beginning of creation, and the "sea of glass" is the reward for all Saints of God who have been through the Tribulation and persecuted while on earth. These once lackluster Christians who were "fence-sitters" now have a mission to either be "hot" for Messiah Yeshua or "cold" for Satan. Once the Tribulation starts, there will be two choices; "hot or cold" No more fence-sitting because the world will be in such distress and turmoil; people will make choices quickly because the antichrist will demand allegiance.

The antichrist is already here on earth demanding allegiance. Many so-called fence-sitting Christians will be "caught up" in the anguish of sin because they were not ready when Yeshua blew His trumpet for the "righteous Saints". The Righteous Saints' reward is to live with the Father for all eternity in peace. No more death or crying. No sin from anyone anymore - we will live a life of love and obedience on earth as it is in Heaven. This is what the Lord's Prayer means.

One day, what is in Heaven will be on earth, and we will live in harmony with everyone. What a marvelous world that will be to finally have family and friends who are loving and kind with the heart of God! We will travel anywhere in the universe once the Millennium begins because the world will be renewed again.

The Tribulation Jews and Gentiles are the ones who come to know Yeshua with harps in hand surrounding the "sea of glass" mingled with fire. After the "gathering," all people left on earth that has endured the Tribulation and come to know Yeshua HaMashiach (Jesus the Messiah) will be ushered into the Kingdom of Almighty God.

The prophecy subject in Matthew 24 regarding Israel starts the seven-year Tribulation up to the end of the three and one-half years. God will "gather up" the consecrated Jews and Gentiles this will occur at the end of the seven years." But who are those standing around the "sea of glass"? Who are these "elect ones"?

When you examine the passage's context, you will see that they are the Jews and Gentiles who will become believers during the Great Tribulation of three and one-half years. This "gathering together" is not the Rapture, though it has several similarities. This gathering of tribulation believers happens after the Great Tribulation, whereas the Rapture of the Church must happen sometime before the beginning of the Great Tribulation and before the antichrist reveals himself in the Temple as "god"."

Our Father God has given us on this earth everything that is needed to have a life of prosperity and fulfillment with the Heavenly realm. And yes, we will work and travel as we do now but with a different purpose. Our mortal bodies will now be immortal and full of righteousness that our fore-parents gave away to Satan. We will now get a chance to fulfill all of the desires that we did not pursue when we were in sin. The numerous careers that we did not pursue and the places we did not travel while on earth will become a reality.

The universe is vast, and we will have the opportunity to explore everything. We will work to better the Kingdom of God and enhance the life that was broken when sin entered our hearts. We will eat from the Tree of Life as stated in Revelation 22:2 (TLV) – "down the middle of the great street of the city. On each side of the river stood the tree of life, bearing twelve kinds of fruit, yielding its fruit every month. And the leaves of the tree were for the healing of the nations."

According to Revelation 22:3, man's curse will be lifted, and we will live with God, and He will live in the city – the New Jerusalem. How glorious this will be, to dwell with the Father in perpetuity. God's name will be written on our foreheads; we will shout and sing praise to God Almighty. There will be no more tears and misery on earth. All the sins will be wiped from our bodies.

We will live in the earthly Garden of Eden that was supposed to be our home before the fall. Remembrance of our lives on earth that were unpleasant will be wiped away; friends, family, and those who were not of God will no longer be recalled in our memory.

Just take a quick trip with me to the pure, righteous Mount of Zion, where we will live in harmony. This is the future of the Christian and Jewish people who confess Messiah Yeshua is

LORD of LORDS and KING OF KINGS. Confession and purification are the start of salvation, and then the change of life-style is the next step. One must continue to be obedient and, most of all, LOVE the Lord God Almighty with your entire heart, mind, Soul, and Spirit.

A Day of Darkness and Gloom

"...a day of darkness and gloom, a day of clouds and blackness. Like dawn spreading across the mountains a large and mighty army comes, such as never was in ancient times nor ever will be in ages to come." (Joel 2:2, NIV)

The "day of darkness and gloom" will be a real event in the near future. The frightening fact; we are so close to the end that we will not recognize the approaching dreadful day of the Lord. "Look up and see Yeshua is coming in the clouds and every eye shall see Him (Rev 1:7, TLV)."

There will be dark menacing clouds, descending from Heaven frightening mankind, our time here on earth will be up, no more chances to repent and live for Yeshua. We are on the verge of an epoch change in our lifestyles, as "time" swiftly moves us to each approaching New Year. Lifestyles will be so radically changed that you will not recognize the coming storm with darkness and dread. We see lifestyles changing daily, as we live in a world of violence, tumultuous evil against everything and everyone. We are on the precipice of the end of the "Church Age," the start of "a day of darkness and gloom" known as the Tribulation.

Salvation can only be found through Yeshua, who resides in people who have given their lives to Christ. A transformation from the old self to a born-again person can be achieved; however, evil is lurking at the door, repent before "time" is up, and the choices will be for Messiah Yeshua or Satan. Once Satan starts his vengeful reign, Gentiles and Jews will be his first victims of choice to devour. Weeping and whaling will be the anguish of mankind. Millions of people will die because the uninformed people who receive all of their news from social media will believe Satan's lie. Who can stand against Almighty God and His wrath when He comes to destroy mankind? Idol worship is at an all-time high around the world. Shopping in stores for worthless items and worshiping modern technology, which God gave the man, has aroused God's anger once again, as it was with the Jews (who were known in ancient times as Hebrews) who prostituted themselves to Ba'al.

John, the Apostle, was in the Spirit (Ruach) when he heard a loud voice behind him that sounded like a trumpet, to write on the scroll (Rev 1:10) what was being shown to him. The voice was Messiah Yeshua telling John to send a message to the seven church communities. These church communities represent all church peoples as they worship Messiah Yeshua, who established, rebuked, commended, and encouraged devoted followers to continue living as faithful followers of Him. Armies from the south will march on Israel; to annihilate them, but HaShem (G-d in Hebrew) will save His chosen people from Satan. The entire world will be involved in World War III, and millions will die for the time of Harvest, of the Grapes has begun for mankind. The Harvest of Grapes means that the wicked and the righteous will die together. The difference will be the wicked will go to Hell, and the righteous will go to Heaven.

Why are so many self-proclaimed Christians sitting idly by watching the Scriptures unfold and doing nothing to save others from the destruction that is coming? My people are sleeping. Scripture says, "My people are destroyed because they lack knowledge of me. Because you rejected that knowledge, I will reject you as a priest for me. Since you forget the Law of your God, I will also forget your children (Hos 4:6, NIV)."

Unfortunately, Christians rarely study or read their Bibles in order to gain more knowledge. People live as if tomorrow will never come, and the revolving door from home to church and back again is just part of the programmed cycle. People live with no thought past the weekly message received during the weekly sermon. There are a few people who actively seek Yeshua during the course of the week, though: Bible study, praise, and worship with other congregants. However, true praise and worship, which lends itself to purification through the study of scripture and absorbing the word of God are rare, in this age of wickedness. No reasonable practice is made to go beyond what is preached. People only seek the Messiah Yeshua when infirmity, life-altering catastrophe strikes their lifestyles; rarely do men seek Yeshua or mention His name? There is a lack of respect for Almighty God, and it starts from birth to death in all mankind.

Men were born with a sin nature derived from the Garden of Eden, where Satan misinterpreted Elohim Adonai's Word to Eve. This direct rebellion opened the door to shame and unworthiness for mankind. The grime of sin covered mankind "immediately" hence sending the entire creation into a tailspin of darkness and gloom.

Retribution had to be executed in order for the Son of God to come and purify mankind from the sin that was committed. The man tried to rectify the sin by sacrificing animals, but this was only a temporary solution that God ordained. He knew the man would rebel against Himself, but Almighty God sent His Son Messiah

Yeshua to be the sacrificial Lamb of God for us, thereby purifying the man so that we could go before the Holy God. This purifying process of the Spirit-led to Saints changing their lives forever, just as Apostle Paul was changed in three days. The three-day anointing process represents Paul's death and rebirth, in the soul and spirit, signifying the death and resurrection of Yeshua. Apostle Paul previously known as Saul, would never be the same after the encounter with Messiah Yeshua. His eyes were opened, after he was blinded, then he started a spiritual revolution of devoted Messianic Jews and Gentiles to bring forth a worldwide movement known as Christianity.

The Eyes of God are everywhere, constantly watching, to see if you will repent of your sin. Some people resolve to repent, and others think they don't have to because they are "good people"; others say, "I was forgiven when Jesus died on the cross so, I don't have to ask for forgiveness." Some folks say, "My name is written in the Book of Life, and I am good and going to Heaven." WRONG! Yes, your name is written in the Book of Life; but, without repentance, you cannot enter into the Kingdom of the El Shaddai (Almighty God).

Scripture is very clear about what you have to do in this life, and if you don't obey the statutes and precepts, you will be cast into darkness where there will be gnashing of teeth. This is Hell-fire away from God, and the light that you thought you were going to see will be darkness. Darkness surrounds souls today, those who half believe in Jesus for what He can give them when they need a quick fix to their repulsive lives. How can you go before Almighty God half-heartily and not know He sees and knows everything about you. The truth is mankind just does not BELIEVE in God. Man does not really care to know God, and He is in the way of what they want to do with their lives.

Satan has planted the lie so deep inside man that it will take a miracle to bring people to the understanding of Jesus Christ. Jesus said very plainly -"Many will say to ME on that day, LORD, LORD, didn't we not prophesy in your name and in your name drive out demons and in your name perform many miracles? Then I will tell them plainly; I never knew you. Away from me, you evildoers! (Matt 7:22-23, NIV)."

Why would God say? "Away from Me"? Man forgets that God can see everything, because He is Omnipresent, Omniscience, and Omnipotent. Ezekiel saw God's glory exit the Temple, and the eyes were on the entire cherubim "...including their backs, their hands, and their wings, were completely full of eyes, as were their four wheels, Ezek 10:12, (NIV)."

These same "four living creatures" are mentioned in Rev 4:8 but they say "Day after day and night after night "Holy, holy, holy is the Lord God, the Almighty." This reference tells you that God is ever-present in the Spirit and never sleeps, as some skeptics have suggested.

The Book of Matthew 7:21, (NIV) also states that "Not everyone who says to me LORD, LORD, will enter the Kingdom of Heaven, but only the one who does the will of my Father who is in Heaven." Ezekiel 33:18-19, (NIV) expounds on the righteous and the wicked and what God expects. It says, "If a righteous person turns from their righteousness and does evil, they will die for it. And if a wicked person turns away from their wickedness and does what is just and right, they will live by doing so."

The word of God cannot be any clearer. REPENTANCE is what ADONAI is requires of all people. To turn from our evil ways so that condemnation will not come upon us. Then the righteous person will be able to live, but if the righteous fail to turn from the wickedness, they will die. "Then they will look toward the earth and see only distress and darkness and fearful gloom, and they will be thrust into utter darkness (Isa 8:22)."

This darkness is Hell. Adonai has made it perfectly clear that you have a choice either with Him and turn away from wickedness or Hell and Satan. In other words, you can be a Christian and go to Hell. Why would you want to go there? Hell is a real place, and the Scriptures speak of this terrible place often, so much so that one cannot mistake the options that are offered to mankind.

Why are there so many sleeping Christians? The old adage that we have time and God is not returning is a myth - people have been saying this for years and centuries. This is the biggest LIE that Satan has supplied in the hearts and minds of Christians or anyone as a matter of fact. Jesus clearly said to His disciples that He would be back, and no one would know the day nor the hour; only the Father knows the exact time. "Look, I come like a thief! Blessed is the one who stays awake and remains clothed so as not to go naked and be shamefully exposed (Rev 16:15, NIV)." This verse not only tells of the exposed soul and spirit but the intent of the heart, which is the nakedness of mankind. Many people will be ashamed when Yeshua returns because they were not ready even though they claimed Yeshua's ownership in public, but the heart was lying. Remember, God is omnipresent and omniscient; He cannot be fooled no matter how much you try to fool yourself that He will not know you have just been caught in the web of Lies the devil has whispered to you.

Let me enlighten you about the parasites that prey on us 24/7; they have been assigned to us to keep our minds on earthly matters. They bring darkness to your soul, and they deposit fabricated words into your soul. The parasitic demon's aim is to distract you from your calling and trick your mind into thinking you are on the right track of life. Deception is their aim as they whisper thoughts of "don't do that" or "you can skip your prayers" or "you don't need to forgive them, they deserve what they got" or a multitude of Lies.

You have to pray away all wickedness from your being. Yeshua had to say to Satan, "It is written" and quoted the Scriptures three times in order to eliminate the evil one from His presence. If

Yeshua had to pray and speak Satan from His presence, then you will have to do the same. The Holy Scriptures are our guidebook to Holy Righteous living, so make sure you read and study it daily for wisdom and understanding. Then ask for wisdom and understanding from Yeshua. It does not appear overnight; this is a gift from Messiah Yeshua that has to be cultivated as you learn to walk according to the word of Almighty God.

Our society has made people insensitive to God, and therefore the signs that are clearly announcing His coming are ignored. America is the country of blessing by God. We have forgotten that our nation was founded on religious freedom, and now we don't see the complete picture anymore; we are totally blind. We allow everything to overshadow our thoughts and mind, thereby never allowing Messiah Yeshua a moment to dwell even for a second to connect with us. We are filthy rags and unfit to go before Almighty God with our wicked hearts, but Jesus gave us an outage to be with Him, that having purification of your heart, repent, and believe in Him then you would be saved.

How are we blind? We are blinded by our greed for more of everything this life has to offer, and we don't care how we get it. We will sell our very souls to get ahead to have more wealth or prestige. Many Americans have never traveled outside of the U.S., so whatever the media selects to transmit is what people believe. Propaganda in the media is the major source of devilment that is purported by the devil. The devil has to lure unsuspecting people, to believe what is seen on electronic devices is real rather than what is known within your heart.

I was once told by a very wise man to verify everything before believing any story. Satan is clearly the deceiver of Mankind, transforming the world into believing that the political and social discriminations of our time are the best way to change the hearts and minds of all people. Unfortunately, people will be led to the slaughter and will take the mark of the beast, because they will believe the LIE and will persuade their Facebook friends that it is "okay" to follow Satan who will be disguised as an angel of light. Just so you know. Satan, known as the deceiver, is already here at work and doing a good job creating chaos in this world. He embodies a real person with the spirit of Satan and will be revealed sooner than you think. I just want you to know that Yeshua is in the chaos and sometimes He creates the chaos to complete His purposes on earth. Yeshua will get the praise and glory.

"Recently a pair of Google looking glasses descended on the world market. What makes these glasses dangerous and even more mind-blowing is the fact the program code is available for free on the creator's website for anyone's use." Since this code is available, anyone with malicious intent could design the glasses to be harmful to mankind. Jesus said, "I am coming soon. Hold on to what you have so that no one will take your crown (Rev 3:11, NIV)."

Numerous Christians will buy these glasses thinking they are okay because they are the new "wave" of technology, and surely they want to have the latest technology so that they can tell or show their friends they are in the "elite crowd." How dangerous this can be for luke-warm Christians. We don't know when God will call us home, and no one knows when the great "gathering" known as the Rapture will take place. We cannot be idly sitting and becoming more conformed to this earth, but be ready to save souls for Christ and be ever mindful of the coming time. "Remember, therefore, what you have received and heard; hold it fast and repent. But if you do not wake up, I will come like a thief, and you will not know at what time I will come to you (Rev 3:3, NIV)."

Today is a time of restoring your life to Christ and facing all fears that have haunted you about who Jesus Christ really is. You cannot know who He is without reading, studying and praying for understanding and wisdom of the Holy Spirit. Incorporating

Jesus into your everyday life is not easy because we are accustomed to doing things on our own and just look at how dysfunctional our lives have turned out. This self-indulgent life was not what Jesus wanted for us. This is why He gave His life so that we could have a life with Him and make our life so rich with godly wisdom.

How do you find peace from within? Peace comes from deep within your Spirit that is given from God to Mankind. In order to receive this peace, you have to become a Christian that is committed to Jesus (Yeshua) in Body, Soul and Spirit. "Peace I leave with you; my peace I give you. I do not give to you as the world gives. Do not let your hearts be troubled and do not be afraid (John 14:27, NIV)."

Jesus gives peace of mind and heart so all you have to do is truly believe in Him and follow with your whole Spirit and Soul. You have to adapt your lifestyle and let go of your old ways of doing things your way and let God lead your life.

So how do you change and become more righteous and not religious?

First, you pray and ask God to lead your life, for example: "Jesus please orders my steps in everything I do this day give me guidance as I go about my daily tasks. Lord, please gives me the wisdom and understanding to follow the Holy Spirit in everything He directs me to do. Lord, what do you have in store for me to do this day, so that I can be successful and prosperous, thereby having favor from you Almighty God. Forgive me of my sins and anything I might have said or done that is not about you."

This would be a prayer to start your relational walk with ADONAI. Make sure to expound more on other areas of your life that need changing. Ask Yeshua to show you what those areas of alteration are and truly work on living a holy life.

Second, you have to sit and be very still and quiet in your Spirit so that you can hear from the Holy Spirit. I guarantee that

He will speak and give you clear and concise guidance now you have to obey and move with God.

Third, thank God for everything that He has done for you during the day and for guiding your steps in the way that you should go.

Fourth, when life is hectic, stop and pray to God as to what you should do about a particular problem or concern, and the Holy Spirit will give you guidance. Sometimes you don't have much time to make decisions, but the Holy Spirit is speaking to you because you asked Him to guide you during the day to listen to that small quiet voice and go with what you know deep within your Spirit is correct. You do have a second to ask God to "help me, Lord." This is all you need, and He will answer your call, and you will make the right choices.

ADONAI is very angry with all nations; HIS wrath is on all their armies. "He will totally destroy them and give them over to slaughter (Isa 34:2)."

Very soon, peace will be taken away from the earth when all righteous Christians and Messianic Jews all over the globe will be taken in the "Rapture or Gathering", then destruction will prevail, and rapid evil will transform the earth into a heaven of satanic evil viler than you could ever imagine. The Holy Spirit will disappear with righteous Christians and Messianic Jews. Those remaining on the earth will be; luke-warm Christians, the 144,000 chosen Jews who will save their people and bring them to Messiah Yeshua; a remnant of believing Jews, non-believing Jews, and sinners who did not give their full life to Messiah Yeshua.

These helpless souls will now have to choose to worship Satan or God. They will look for comfort from a cold edifice that looms in the skies with no God-given Spirit to ease the pain of loss that will be felt without God. You cannot imagine what this earth will be like - you think it is awful now, but there is a restraining that

God has provided until He gathers His people unto Himself. That restraining is the Holy Spirit.

Almighty God will put His mark on His own people, and they will be spared the wrath, this is the "elect Jews"; this is not for luke-warm Christians that are left or non-believing Jews who have strayed unto Baal. There will be people who will not be transformed because they will not have the heart of God. Scripture states, "for the mystery of lawlessness are already at work. Only He who now restrains it will do so until he is out of the way (2 Thess 2:7, NIV)."

If you want to wait and see how it will be on earth after the Rapture, it will be too late because scripture says that "for this reason, God sends them a powerful delusion so that they will believe the lie (2 Thess 2:11, NIV)."

This is very "scary" to know that God will send a delusion just as Nebuchadnezzar was full of pride and brought down to the dirt of the earth after his reign and admission that he built and reigned over the Jews. Read the book of Daniel in the Bible.

There has been a vigorous discussion about a Rapture-ready Church for centuries as to whether the Church would be gathered to Yeshua; Pre-Tribulation, Mid-Tribulation, or Post Tribulation. The discussion comes from a verse of scripture in 2 Thessalonians 2:1, (TLV), where it states "...the coming of the Lord Jesus Christ and our gathering together to Him..." this scripture has spun exuberant debate and arguments among Theologians; Rabbis, and Christians more than anything else besides the belief that Jesus Christ is the true Messiah.

I have had discussions with people who have Theologian Doctorate degrees or non-degrees, and no one had a definitive answer. I got fed-up with the numerous answers and decided to ask Almighty God to explain and teach me what was really written about His coming. I had a very wise Grandmother who taught me scripture at age five. She was a Missionary and Theologian who

21

traveled throughout the state of North Carolina. She did not go to seminary school but was taught by the Holy Spirit. She read extensively since she was a certified school teacher and a very wise and righteous person. She advised me always to ask questions of God, and He would give me the answers I sought.

I asked God myself, and He answered me - after I had done abundant study from Hebrew writings, Hebrew scripture, and prayer. This is my belief and opinion. You will only know "truth" if we are alive when Yeshua comes before, or during, or after, the Tribulation. Jesus does not know when He is coming; therefore, you will not know. But be ready and continue to bring salvation to the world. According to scripture, Yeshua will gather the Rapture-ready Church before the Tribulation. The Church will not go through the Tribulation in which God will pour out His judgment wrath on an unbelieving world (1 Thess.1:10; 4:13–18; 5:4-11, TLV). The Apostle Paul determined that the "Day of the Lord" would not come prior to the Rapture (2 Thess).

How foolish it will be to wait until He comes and then forsakes the Messiah Yeshua and sells your Soul to the devil. Preparing people to see the real light of Jesus Christ has become a daunting task for fully committed Christians. The scripture from Revelation is very eerie for fence-sitting Christians because their task is to lead others to Christ after the Rapture.

How can you lead someone to Christ when you don't know the scriptures yourself and have doubts that the creator of the World really exists? You might know scripture or go to church, but when you truly don't believe, then you are on the precipice to fall into Hell. I am not trying to scare you, but something should scare you and not a scary movie which is not real. Your very Soul is at risk, and this is for eternity, not just for a year or so, but forever and ever!

You cannot be sure that your heart will not be hardened and thereby lose your Soul. Connecting with the Prince of Peace now is the only sure way to help dying souls. He is waiting for committed men and women of God to come forth and give their lives to Yeshua before it is too late. Signs have been in the Heavens and on earth of Yeshua's coming, yet you just think everything is "awesome" and so you tweet, "God is not real or worthy of your time." WRONG! Our very Souls are in travail. There are only two choices to make Heaven or Hell, and the default is HELL.

We witnessed two Blood Moons in 2014 and two in 2015. These blood moons had a meaning for the Jewish nation. However, they were not an omen, as some folks have purported.

"ALL four blood moons occurred on major Jewish holidays! The blood moon occurred on Passover 2014, followed by the holiday of Sukkot 2014. On Passover 2015, another blood moon occurred, and then again on Sukkot 2015. This has happened only eight times in all of history! "And there's even more! Major events of significance to the Jewish people happened on each of the last three recorded times that these rare blood moons occurred. They were events that changed the course and direction of Jewish history for all time."

"Believers around the world of diverse faiths are attributing the blood moon phenomenon to the teaching of the prophet Joel, who had preached: I will set wonders in the heavens and the earth: blood and fire and pillars of smoke; the sun will turn to darkness and the moon to blood before the coming of the great and awesome Day of God (Joel 3:3)."

Inspired by the concluding words of Joel, some are suggesting that the blood moons are a sign from God that we are one step closer to the coming of the Messiah. The hype of the four blood moons was just that hype. What did occur was more anti-Semitic terror attacks caused many Jews to take pause and consider going to the homeland of Israel? The terror attacks spread rapidly across many countries, and of course, the United States was the biggest culprit of racial hate. "Nevertheless, the words of the Talmud can give you some insight on how we should relate to all possibilities and speculations: When the Jews perform the will of God, they need not worry about omens [or celestial phenomenon]. Thus say the Lord, "Do not be frightened by the signs of the heavens. (Talmud Sukkah 29a) The words of Rabbi Ari Enkin will shine new light on what will happen in future days. Blood Moons has always coincided with Major Jewish Holidays. This alone is a sign from God."

With events scoring at a supersonic rate in the world, you have to be prepared to find God and save souls. Struggling to find happiness on earth is not what you should be doing; this fleshly concept is not of God. People wait until they are in their 60s, 70s, 80s, or 90s to ask the question, "why I am still here, and what does God want me to do?" The quick answer is you can continue to save your family members and be a beacon of light to everyone you meet. You have so much wisdom to give, and you cannot just sit around and think about your ailments and go into a comatose state of disbelief because you are not improving the Kingdom of God if you are stagnating.

We all have a job to do, and until we breathe our last breath on this earth, we can save someone from the very pit of Hellfire. Whether you want to believe it or not, Hellfire is very real, and the Bible mentions it frequently "don't say, I don't want to hear this." I just want you to know that it is real, and every human should research the scriptures and know that God is not playing with them. God is REAL, and He has a designated time for everyone to complete their mission on earth, and if you miss it, then there is no chance to redeem your life once you are dead. This is a fact. Get going and find peace and God.

The Blood and Water

"Messiah Yeshua is the One who came by <u>water</u> and <u>blood</u>—not by water only, but by <u>water and blood</u>. The Spirit is the One who testifies, because the Spirit is the truth." (1 John 5:6, TLV)

There is a song that says "Oh, the blood of Jesus" this song speaks of how the blood that was shed by Yeshua on the cross will purify your Spirit and Soul. The blood of our Holy Jesus cleansed our sinful bodies, and the water of baptism cleansed our fleshy spiritual bodies to be prepared to serve. This is why you are baptized so that the Holy Spirit can come and live inside you, but you have to be washed (purified) in the water first. You have to be prepared to sacrifice your life for Jesus and go through trials and tribulations.

The water emersion represents the humbling of your fleshy body and Soul to be prepared to receive the holiness of Jesus and the holiness of the Holy Spirit (Ruach HaKodesh). No mortal man can enter into the holiness of the Triune God without being cleansed of all unrighteousness. Your preparation after emersion opens the door for you to eat the bread and wine which signifies the renewing of the Soul and Spirit of Jesus and His Father, Holy God.

This sacrificial moment is a reminder of Messiah Yeshua's shed blood on the cross in His flesh for all mankind for their vile sins forever. He became the sacrificial lamb so that there would never be animal sacrifices again because you would have to constantly put animals on the altar in order to bring about repentance. Messiah Yeshua went to the altar for us by dying and was raised in three days to return to His Father, Almighty God and now sits in Heaven on the right-hand of Elohim Adonai. We are now purified so that is why we pray to Yeshua through the Holy Spirit so that we now have an advocate in Heaven who prays for us and acknowledges our prayers provided they are not selfish prayers or un-holy prayers. The Ruach HaKodesh is a Spirit who hears and gives you advice when you ask and when you don't ask. He is that voice that says "don't do that" so you should thank Him for your life and thank Him for helping you daily to get through your life. Remember HaShem (God) is comprised of three spiritual beings; Father God, Father Son, and Father Holy Spirit.

Adonai has planned fire and suffering for mankind those who choose not to believe in Him. HE will send the 10 plagues of Egypt but this time it will be seven times more severe. EL Shaddai (Lord God Almighty) sent the Ruach HaKodesh (Holy Spirit) the water and the blood these three are One. Once you understand who Adonai really is then you will understand the full meaning of the Spirit, water, and the blood.

Many devout Christians are praying that Adonai spares the earth from the coming Tribulation and torment but the man has not worshiped God and they have made His earth an abomination worse than Sodom and Gomorrah. Men are so proud that they don't care about the earth, animals, vegetation, the atmosphere, or their very lives. All man wants is to show what they have made out of stone, metal, and nonsensical things that don't bring awareness of God.

The earth belongs to Elohim Adonai because He is our Creator and He created the world. Foolish man has allowed Satan to cloud our minds and blind our eyes. Many of the elect (Jews) have gone over to Satan and his lies; this is why there will be a day of sorrow coming that no man will be able to survive the agony. HaShem has a remnant that is true to Him, and they are seeking to save as many from Holy God's wrath as possible and they are urgently seeking God's face they are the Messianic Jews and committed Gentile Christians. Many people will die because of their sins, disobedience, and reluctance to serve God. People have found the possessions of this earth to be more enticing than knowing God. Their idolized possessions have allowed them to prostitute themselves to get more and more devices and possessions to the point of violence. Man would rather die for these gadgets rather than talk to God. All they want is to satisfy their flesh which is graving more sinful contraptions of this wicked world. God's patience has worn out and He is coming sooner than you think or could imagine.

The prayers of the righteous have gone up to Almighty God in the Heavens and He has heard their words and aware of their suffering. However, there is a spiritual awakening taking place on earth with the youth, and the more seasoned Christians that is making the difference, so that mature Christians can save as many as possible before the "gathering of the Saints." God knows most people don't believe in the gathering of the Saints, but His Word is true and He has put everything in the scriptures for mankind to study and interpret, provided we ask for God's wisdom and understanding. This pre-tribulation and post-tribulation are nonsense because God's Word strictly states that He will gather His people to be with Him. There will be seven years of Tribulation. During that time God will gather the 144 thousand to a safe place, where His marks will be put on them to save the chosen people. He will take committed Christians and Messianic Jews to Heaven with Him and we will have a glorious banquet in Heaven.

Why is Almighty God's word not read and translated correctly? Ancient Translators did not look to the Jewish writing as the true gospel; they decided to change the Hebraic words from the scrolls to fit their own requirements thinking that people who could not read during the ancient's time would not know if the scriptures from the Jewish writing were altered. This was another trick of Satan to confuse the Saints and the ethnic Jews. In modern times anthropologists have discovered that the ancient "dead sea scrolls" have been found to be true and unaltered. The book of Isaiah is exactly as translated today as it was in ancient times except for a few word changes.

I have discerned through study, the few word changes made in the English textual version of the Bible makes a difference in how we read the Scripture and how the Hebrew, Latin or Greek is translated from the original language to the English version. A Hebrew word in a sentence can mean two to eight different meanings in a sentence. You have to look at the entire sentence and pray to get the correct translation or search for a Hebraic translation in the original language. This is not what the average person will do; only the committed Christian will seek more knowledge and understanding. Remember your pastor or rabbi cannot give you comprehensive explanations to Yeshua's word in a weekly sermon. You have to seek and study the Scriptures to acquire truth for yourself.

I have discovered many verses in the English King James to be different in English than what is written in the Hebrew Bible or Tanakh. Let's be clear there is no Old Testament for the Jews, it is called the Tanakh and it has divisions: Torah, Nevi'im (Prophets), and Ketuvim (writings). Thereby the meaning of a sentence will take on a new life if translated correctly from the Hebrew to the

English. I still believe us as Christians should have learned Hebrew when we were younger, thereby learning to translate the Word of Holy God correctly and we would have a clearer knowledge of God and His Hebrew Language. We will all speak Hebrew in Heaven so if you know the language now, you will have a pre-knowledge of Hebrew for the after-life.

There are times when you read the Scripture you feel as if there is something missing. English translators decided to ignore critical facts in the Bible because they decided it was not necessary to go further into the explanation regarding the Nephilim (the Giants). One example, the truth about the "fallen angels" having relations with the women on earth found in Genesis 6:1-4 is fraught with multiple questions. The Nephilim who walked on earth as men of renown is a historical fact because documentation has been found on various archeological exhibitions throughout the world. There is one paragraph mentioned about the Nephilim as far as the written Biblical Scriptures is concerned. However, the Nephilim is throughout the Old Testament so they were real but the explanation as to how they came about is a mystery. So who were the Nephilim? What really happens to the women is my question? I had to read the Parashah (Weekly Tanakh) in English to discover the truth about the Giants. I had to read the Midrash commentaries for explanations beyond to really get the truth and then an extensive study of older writings before I was able to find "truth." Even though some of the Scriptures are missing, if the translators have put in everything from the Holy Scriptures most people would not have read the Bible anyway. People have a tendency to not read the Bible, and what is already written in the Bible, is too excessive for the average person to comprehend all at once.

If Jehovah God had given all of the books and all of the information all at once no one would have read the Bible for understanding. Additional, information that could be researched was meant for the scholarly mature Christian who seeks God's face. All Jehovah God has wanted is for mankind to seek His face, honor, and worship Him rather than the things their hands have made. He has given us the knowledge to make appropriate choices - yet we don't acknowledge Jehovah, but we acknowledge Satan as our father.

Jehovah God loves mankind, however; the chaos that is pervading in the world is not Jehovah God's doing. He is allowing the deceiving spirit to scheme, through deception to fulfill the Holy Scriptures. Almighty God sent a deceiving spirit to Micaiah the Prophet against King Ahab according to 2 Chronicles 18:20-21,(NIV), *"Then a spirit came forward and stood before the LORD and said, 'I will entice him.' And the LORD said to him, 'How?' "He said, 'I will go and be a deceiving spirit in the mouth of his prophets.' Then He said, 'You are to entice him and prevail also. Go and do so.'"*

If we would just stop and read God's Holy word, thus meditate, pray, ask for wisdom, and understanding then we would be astute students of the Holy Scriptures and prepared for worldly rebellion. It is not complicated to gain wisdom, but unpretentious. HaShem is preparing all people to meet their eternity or their demise. Whatever is their choice? The man was given a brain to choose who they would serve, but unfortunately, the sin from our Father Adam gave us the wrong recipe to life. The life mankind chose was a sinful path. The path of sin is so wide and many people are on this highway. As a matter of fact, it is so crowded that the road had to be expanded to accommodate the number of people on the road. The road to Elohim Adonai is so narrow that few are on the road. The simple fact that you go to church does not guarantee you will have a home in Heaven.

HaShem (God) wishes His Servants of the cloth would stop preaching that LIE in the pulpits. HaShem knows your heart. Many so-called Christians sit in church every week, and they are full of the Devil and their hearts are far from God. Their faces tell the story if you are to look deep into them because they don't want to give up their fleshly lives and live for God.

People only pray to God when they are in a dilemma, but when a truly heartfelt prayer really counts to ascend to Heaven man blames God for their plummeting lives and get angry at God. The anger is so intense that you entirely stop acknowledging Almighty God whereby blaming HIM for reducing your luxurious life to oblivion. This miserable existent happens with jobs not obtained, health issues, family loss of life, broken marriages, political destruction and the list is endless. You cannot worship two masters; you either hate one or honor the other.

Once you select the life you really want to live then do it and stop playing Church. Remember, Messiah Yeshua knows your heart and HE sees everything you are doing? This reality concept of an Omnipresent, Omniscience God scares people. To assume that an invisible Spirit known as Elohim Adonai can discern your thoughts and can see what you are doing is a false reality to the masses of people on earth. This concept is not understood, and it is a mystery to most people and to get the true appreciation of what God wants is to be knowledgeable about HIM. The righteous Saints of ancient times had faith and were commended as righteous because they were *purified* and had *faith*. They did not have the distractions of modern-day Saints. Yet they had to work their fields and fight off surrounding enemies daily, they did not waivers in their faith as Hebrews 11 speaks of the mighty ancients.

Let me get to the meat of this discussion. The heart and brain are connected to the Spirit of man. They are linked and when a heart or brain is taken out of one man and put into another that is wrong. Mankind thinks this is great because someone has been saved but the heart and brain are the control center of man, the blood of man this is what makes man live or die. If you take the heart and the brain then put it into another then the person who receives it will have symptoms of the one who died because that heart or brain is connected to the blood of the giver, it was not meant for the receiver. Again man is playing God.

It is wonderful that man has saved so many people but when it comes to the heart and brains those organs should be left alone. If the person was not saved and the one who receives those organs is saved then believers in Messiah Jesus will have correlations with the unsaved person and the body will reject the organs. If both were unsaved then, the body would receive the organs. However, the recipient will always have symptoms from its recipient because of the blood connection.

The Spirit is now a part of the living person. Scientists will argue with me, but a Christian doctor or scientist will understand this concept of your body. The body was made for you and when the DNA and tissues are altered there will be consequences. There are many other religions including Orthodox Jews, Native Americans, South Asia Muslims, and the Catholic Church who do not believe in organ donor-ship just to name a few. There are many Christian believers who think otherwise and advocate donating these organs, but they have not understood the real concept of organ donor-ship from a Biblical standpoint. I am sure people will disagree with me. This is my opinion and belief like my Jewish and Ethiopian brothers and sisters who believe that you do not mutilate the body.

During these last days on earth, Mankind will find that God's grace and mercy are almost gone and the cup of mercy is nearly empty and the cup of iniquity is full and running over. Almighty God has placed His Warrior Angels among the remnants that will prepare those people who want to know Jehovah God before HIS arrival. A vast number of souls worldwide of all ethnicity and religious backgrounds are seeking Jehovah God because of HIS appearing to them in dreams and visions. They are not aware at first it is Messiah Yeshua, but Messiah Yeshua will either appear to them or send them a true Saint of God who has His heart, to hear the Word and they will become believers in Messiah Yeshua.

Yeshua wants to save everyone, however not all people will be saved and repent, because the world has enticed so many Christians. Christians have become worldly, and all they want is the things that the earth can give them which are beautiful things, easy living, and money. The fabulous living is the way of the Western world which has corrupted so many other countries into believing the lie from Satan. All of God's transformed children have come to know that the easy life is not real.

God's word states that trouble will come to His children and we will be tested and tried by fire and will emerge purified Saints ready for all assignments that are put before us. Without tribulation, we would not be able to approach Messiah Yeshua and Adonai in Heaven. Your heart has to be righteous without guile or fault. You have to know that Elohim Adonai is the Supreme Creator and your Father; He only wants the best for you. This thought of getting rich and having all of the things of the earth is a "false" religion. Yes, you will have the things that God wants for you, and you will not want for anything. But to live like you are a very rich person is not what God requires. HE wants a true walking, talking, praying, and believing relationship with HIM that cannot be manufactured but authentic.

As the scriptures spoke about the very rich man in the Bible, he could not come to know Yeshua, because he could not give up the things of the earth to hear Yeshua's calling. You have to give up the fleshly things before you approach Yeshua. Now, if that means giving up what you already have acquired then do that. You see the real meaning is to give Yeshua what is already HIS. HE has given us homes, food, money, and health. The money is Messiah Yeshua's so He requires that you give only a tenth of what you earn to Him, to help those in need and to build up the church collectively so that all will benefit from your wealthy earnings.

Not to be a Robin Hood defector to rob from the poor and give to the rich. Not that He wants you to live as a pauper, but as a man focused on God and not on man-made articles. If you only see what your hands have made and a horde all of those material belongings and not care to give it away then you will get back what you give out and that is nothing. My Dad and Mom always told me to "cast your bread upon the water, and you will get an abundance back." (Ecc1:1) You have to give unselfishly to God with your whole heart with sincerity, and then He will know you are giving not to be seen by the world but with love.

Just as Ananias and Sapphira contributed to "The Way" (first name of Christians) and held back monies after stating, they gave everything to the church. They would have lived as Christians for the church if they had been truthful with their offerings. Instead, they held back some of the money; therefore, Yeshua killed Ananias and Sapphira, because they Lied to the Holy Spirit. Their heart was evil and not righteous. They did not ask Messiah Yeshua if they could keep some of the monies to live on. Ananias and Sapphira lied and hid the monies and presented only a small stash of their income thinking, Yeshua would not know what they had done. "You see I SEE EVERYTHING THAT IS DONE. I AM THAT I AM! Nothing is hidden from me." ADONAI'S word says in (Jeremiah 16:17, 2 Chronicles 25:2, "my eyes see everything" 2 Chronicles 16:9 "For the eyes of the LORD run throughout the earth." Stay connected to God, purify your body, mind, and Spirit and you will see the Heavenly place in the Rapture or Gathering.

Chapter 2

Salvation

War-Weary Christians – The Coming Prophecy

"*A MAN MAY HIDE FROM HIMSELF, AND YET HE CANNOT hide himself from God.*" *William Secker (d.1681?)*

"*Now when Solomon finished praying the fire came down from heaven and consumed the burnt offering and the sacrifices, and the glory of Adonai filled the House. The kohanim could not enter into the House of Adonai because the glory of Adonai filled the House of Adonai.*" *(2 Chronicles 7:1-2, TLV)* (Kohanim=priests) (House=temple)

WAR-WEARY CHRISTIANS HAVE FORGOTTEN that our battles are fought on our knees in prayer and we have to have the correct armament to fight the devil and his minions. If we are constantly fighting our battles with our flesh, then we will wear down quickly and have nothing left for Messiah Jesus. Society has determined that everything is centered on electronic devices that have one purpose in mind, that is, to thwart mankind into the schemes and traps of Satan, who uses the devices to keep us busy with irrational judgments.

Christians have found themselves so war-weary with wars on every front with every neighborhood and country that there is nowhere to run or hide. Just stepping out of your door every day has become a battle zone for most people though-out the world. If you are not of God then, you are battling the Saints; if you are battling the Saints then, you are a demonized person, with one thing on your mind to destroy all Christians, Jews/Messianic Jews. The weak fence-sitting Christians, who have not fully given their hearts to Jesus Christ, sit in church and pretend they are listening to the word of God. They pretend to be slain in the spirit or fall out and wail all for a show. This performance level of spirituality is known as "I got my praise on" is a display for the audience. It is befitting to praise God and actually feels the Holy Spirit, but to announce to your friends, that the spectacle was a show is a demonized spirit. If you don't announce that you "got your praise on", but you display the same hateful person in the flesh - when you leave the worship service is evidence that performance you gave in worship service was an act. God knows it and you know it and that is a huge sin in Messiah Yeshua's eyes. The fence-sitting Christian will say and perform the entire Christian-ease lingo, yet their heart is bent on evil. Just as soon as the service is over or before they leave the church they are talking about someone, not speaking to people, rude by pushing to get out of a church, or speaking out loud - to discredit a person all for what? Just to be a wicked selfish person not knowing their soul is headed to Hell.

Salvation came to the holy elect of Adonai when the temple of Adonai was built by Solomon. Adonai gave a stern warning to Solomon if the Jews turn away and forsakes the decrees and commands He had given; then they would be uprooted from Israel, the land that Adonai gave them and He would reject the temple that was consecrated for His Name.

Historically the Jews in the Scriptures ensued their old ways of idol worship, consequently losing the temple again and were scattered throughout the world as a punishment that has lasted until modern times. The Jewish people are now moving back to their homeland in droves from all nations in the world. God promised to bring them back even though they were disobedient; this was still His chosen people. We can learn so much from our Jewish cousins as to how to really worship Adonai and be obedient people of all nationalities.

The books of Leviticus and Ezekiel describe the temple architectural plan as well as how the Jews were to worship and live before Adonai. Righteous mankind will live in harmony one day and will be surrounded by God's divine light and power with new concentrated bodies. Transformed men will be established as holy before the face of God, just as the Jewish people were when the temple was built by Solomon. When the fire came down from Heaven, the people worshiped because they were in awe of a Holy and Righteous God who was a consuming fire. The intensity of this event was so awesome; they could not look up to Adonai for they were not worthy. The people had temporally learned to be obedient in the presence of Holy Adonai. The Levitical priests could not go into the temple because they would have died in the presence of Adonai. Scripture states "that no man can come into the presence of God and live (Ex 33:20)."

The sons (Nadab and Abihu (Leviticus 10)) of Aaron the Priest were killed by God because they came into His presence with unauthorized fire with an offering that was not *sacrificed* and *purified*. They put fire in their censers and added incense then offered it before Adonai. In addition, they had drunk wine in the tent, which put them in rebellion toward Almighty God. They were burned to death in front of their father Aaron with the strange fire that they presented before the Lord. Fire came down from Heaven and consumed the men clothes and all. They had to be dragged out of the "tent of meeting" with their clothes on that were buried.

The lesson to be learned; do not go before the Lord unpurified and unsanctified with sin. You have to repent of your sins before you can go before God otherwise, He will not hear your earnest prayer of forgiveness. All men have fallen short in their lives to live holy; therefore, they cannot enter the Kingdom of God without repentance. In 1 Corinthians 6:9-11, (NIV) says "Do not be deceived: Neither the sexually immoral, nor idolaters, nor adulterers, nor men who submit to or perform homosexual acts, nor thieves, nor the greedy, nor drunkards, nor verbal abusers, nor swindlers, will inherit the Kingdom of God."

It states that you were washed and *sanctified* and justified in the Name of Jesus and by the Holy Spirit. We are always told that God loves us and that is true. You have to remember that Elohim Adonai is a Spirit and not a mortal man. He is to be revered, honored, respected, loved and obeyed at all times. When we are disobedient, there are consequences and they are severe. Just as a child is disobedient to a parent or in society there are severe consequences, so we must expect Holy Omnipotent God to have the same rules and regulations.

How do we obtain *Salvation*? Salvation comes when you have a yearning in your heart, to know there is someone in the universe that has control over your life, and this Spirit Being is called God, and He has made this vast world. The meaning of salvation according to the online dictionary is [1]"preservation or deliverance from harm, ruin, or loss." The Latin word is from salvare which means to save. One can deduce that salvation can be achieved by faith in Jesus the Holy Lamb of God. A true belief in Jesus exists currently and forever, transforming Him into a complete image, of the Triune God-Head.

How do you really get *salvation*? There is always something that yearns inside your inner man that says "is this all there is to life?" When you get to that point in life and your life has no meaning. You have accomplished all or some of the goals you have set, yet you are still unfulfilled. Maybe you have accomplished nothing and feel lost and feed-up with life and afraid of your future, because it has no beginning and no end. This is when you are ripe for Satan to discourage your inspirations for goodness with evil wicked schemes. You start searching for answers to other religions and find that they too lack that true sense of fulfillment. You hear the "still small voice say", I am here for you and I will never leave you, lie or reject you, for if I do reject you, I reject Myself and I made you from the dirt of the earth. Whatever you decide to do, don't give up on your life. Stay focused on positive things in your life, even when you cannot see the positive. Many people throughout the world have become great; because they first had nothing, but the fortitude to forge ahead to become a living example of success, despite all odds against them in this world is a true testament for Jesus. Having a positive attitude and the drive to be the best that you can be and help others on your journey is a Christ-like spirit.

Now the "still small voice" of Yeshua may not articulate quite like I have written it, but believe me, you will hear from God. Now there is another voice that will be similar. You have to be very careful the spirit of Satan comes as light also and have fooled many non-Christians and Christians alike into sin and damnation. Satan will be very crafty by saying "did you really hear from God" or "you can make quick money with drugs, gambling, or other ungodly ventures." Your Spirit will emit a signal to your heart that these ventures are not from Yeshua. Sometimes people that are non-Christian call this signal your conscience. We all have a conscience that works with the Holy Spirit, but this is somewhat deeper in worth if you are a Christian. That deep "churning in your stomach" is your Spirit imparting the truth to you letting you know a big mistake is about to happen if you listen to the voice of perdition. Those that are not of God have their conscience giving them a signal that something is wrong; however, many ignore the indicator. The Holy Scripture says to, "test the spirit." This suggests one must ask God to confirm in His word, the answers you seek if you are a Christian. If you are a non-Christian, ask Jesus to help you with the problem or steer your dreary life into the fullness that He has promised for you. Yeshua has given you the Holy Spirit, He will communicate the acceptable manner on how to live your life, thereby life will be exciting and complete.

Make sure you are truly quiet and seeking Jesus so you can hear Him and see the "sign" that He sends. Sometimes it happens fast and quick, other times Yeshua takes His time, while He is molding you into a righteous person, He wants you to be during your sanctification molding period. Once you come into the knowledge that Yeshua is really Jesus the Holy Lamb of God, and He was with His Father when the universe and man were created, then you will be on your way to becoming a "friend of God." Your next step is to find a Bible teaching Jesus/Yeshua believing church or Messianic Congregation, and then you are on your way to having a relationship with Almighty God because you will start the Biblical learning process with other Christians.

Who is Man that he can determine his own destiny? Who is Man that he can hide from what God has ordained for the world and for individuals? We were made from the red dirt of the earth, yet we will find that we can only do what God has ordained in the Spirit for us to achieve on this earth. We mask the truth about what is coming in this new church age, and we assume a lot of things about what the scriptures actually say. God said He has had prophets write down what to expect and still man is unwilling to believe even the simplest of "truth" that is written in "plain" English. God knows what He can do and man cannot tell Him, when He is coming back for His own Church or what He will be doing before His appearing, remember He is "I AM that I AM (Exodus 3:4)."

People will say. "He is here" or "He is there" but He is still in Heaven aggressively looking at wicked the man and their ignorance of Him. Romans 1:18, (NIV) says "the wrath of God is being revealed from heaven against all the Godlessness and wickedness of people, who suppress the truth by their wickedness. . ." God is very angry and heart-broken with what is happening on earth, but it is no surprise to Him. He has "special agents" known as salvation seeking Christians or Messianic Jews who are moving with the Spirit of God to save the unholy. Messiah Yeshua's Father, Elohim Adonai cannot stand the sight of the man in these mortal bodies; because he has defiled His sanctuary on earth, with the corruption of all fleshly thoughts and actions. This is why Yeshua said, He would bear our sins and came to earth as a human, died, was buried, arose from the dead, and sits at the right-hand of His Father so that we could go before Elohim Adonai.

Nahum 1:2-3, (NIV) states that "The LORD is a jealous and avenging God; the LORD takes vengeance and is filled with wrath. The LORD takes vengeance on his foes and vents His wrath against his enemies. The LORD is slow to anger but great in power; the LORD will not leave the guilty unpunished. His way is in the whirlwind and the storm, and clouds are the dust of his feet." Remember, God said that He is governing and He is the Creator of everything. Do not play with God, Gal 6:7, (NIV), "Do not be deceived: God cannot be mocked. A man reaps what he sows."

He is coming sooner than later. The only reason Messiah Yeshua has not come is to save more souls before the great "gathering" of His people from this earth. I have never experienced the anger of God as I have in these sections of the Holy Scriptures. A must-read is the books of Ezekiel, Daniel, Isaiah, Revelation, and Hosea to name a few of my favorites. Scripture says. "Look up your redemption is near (Luke 21:28)." I am the Alpha and the Omega, the First and the Last, the Beginning and the End (Rev

41

22:13, NIV)." Those who follow Gods commandments and statues will be raptured (gathered up) when He sends His Son Jesus Christ. Jesus (Yeshua) will judge the earth and its inhabitants.

A strange verse appears in Matthew 22:12-13, (TLV) about the "Wedding Garment." It references the righteous, and the wicked is invited to the "wedding banquet." People who are true believers in their heart will put on the garment and accept Jesus as their Lord and Savior regardless of their station in life. Those who do not accept Jesus will be cast into darkness where there will be wailing and gnashing of teeth. Verse 12 states: "but the unfaithful heirs of that kingdom will be thrown into the darkness outside. In that place, there will be wailing and gnashing of teeth. Tie him up hand and foot and throw him into outer darkness. For many are called, but few are chosen." Yeshua asks the man the following question; *"Friend, he said to him, how did you get in here without wedding clothes? But the man was silent."* This man did not come into the kingdom by faith, but by pretending to be one of the faithful. His clothes were filthy rags, and he did not put on the offered righteous clothes, nor did he accept Jesus as his Savior. Therefore, he was questioned by Yeshua and he was lacked in faith and was condemned by not answering, then he was gagged and bound and then cast into utter darkness. This is how life will be in the "last days" many will say, "I preached in your name and gave to the poor," but they never confessed their sins and truly because a witness for Yeshua, consequently, their silence will be their damnation.

"Listen, I tell you a great mystery: We will not all sleep, but we will all be changed, in a flash, in the twinkling of an eye, at the last trumpet. For the trumpet will sound, the dead will be raised imperishable, and we will be changed (1 Cor 15:51-52, NIV)."

We have massacred babies and killed each other for no apparent reason, so where would such evil come from? It would only come from Satan who is still trying to get as many people under his control before his time is up. How does man not understand this? They cannot understand because they are under the influence of this world and all it has to offer, just as Satan offered the world to Jesus (Yeshua) when He was in the wilderness for 40 days.

Living a life of sin without repentance will only send you to Hell. Time is short, and we don't recognize the urgency of this statement. Just look at the world and how people are running to other countries to get away from evil. No peace can be found or rest for weary bodies or souls. Countries are turning away people, and many are Christians dying in the Mediterranean Sea or between countries where foreign governments have placed scores of people in what was once a concentration camp or in slave camps.

My heart is weary, and my prayers are numerous for the Saints of God who are suffering. When will persecution stop? Unfortunately, it is just getting started and will get much worse until Messiah Yeshua comes and regulates the earth to its original form. Satan has not been fully released as of yet once the Antichrist appears to look out, Jews and those Saints left that did not give their whole heart to Messiah Yeshua (fence-sitting Christians), you will be persecuted beyond reason.

The Saints of God and Messianic Jews will have to leave before the full intensity of evil will start, and of course, God's wrath will be swift and deadly, for those who refused to acknowledge Him and proceed to take the mark of the Beast. More people will go to Hell than you can imagine. It is time for righteous Christians to get their house in order for the time of portraying church or no church or having a relationship with God or not with God is over. Once God takes you out of this world it is over; you cannot **"repent"** your life just Hellfire. As I have stated in my previous book *"Just the Edge of God,"* we have a destiny and God made us worship Him and not the things of this world. So many distractions have made us forget why we are here on this magnificent earth.

There is one bright light for those who are left behind (fence-sitting Christians) there will be a revival from the Jewish people the 144,000 wills save many people in the world once the Church has been "gathered." There will be a time of repentance of sins and renewing of life to Adonai and His Son Messiah Yeshua. However, the door of opportunity will be very short and difficult for people to be delivered into the kingdom of Messiah Yeshua because Satan will have full control over the earth and over your mind.

People make promises to God that they cannot keep yet they pretend to pray for the sick and shut-in. More excuses can be found when it comes to tithes and offerings, people cannot give their full tithes to the church since their mouths are full of selfishness and many lies from Satan. The excuses as to why a Christian cannot give a tenth of their money are worrisome and the constant complaining is beyond sinful, it is ridiculous.

Satan really achieved his goal to distract mankind from things of God to senseless possessions. When you see people pull out their cell phones to text, Snapchat, Facebook, playing games on the cell phone or checking their Instagram account during a worship service, or even worse sleeping in the pew and knitting in church while the sermon is being preached is an abomination to God. Constant talking is an interruption in the service as well as snoring when you should be "praising God."

Why come to church if your heart is not into it. It is better to go to Hell than to participate in the service. The pastor cannot get you into the mood, neither nor the praise choir. You should come to the Temple of God ready to bow before your Creator, who is awesome in His wonderment. All of your praise should be every day not just on Sabbath or Sunday. Your very breath is from Jesus

Christ because you are a "mist in the air" and can be snuffed out quickly.

The Church is not a social club or a nightclub where the music for church is from the club down the street. Jazz-like music and drinking, all in the name of the church is an abomination toward Adonai; those who participate will pay dearly with their lives going through Hellfire. The music should be a praise tune that reflects God, not the club, or the latest R&B tune that was reworded to be played in a church praise service.

When will we become the Christians of Peter and Paul? They were seriously seeking Messiah Jesus and wanting to learn more by reading and studying their Bibles or Tanakh during their era. That means your attention should be on praise and worship and not the technology that is in your hands. Your mind should be on God and how to make your life better and accept Jesus as your Lord and Savior. So if you are just a lump of clay sitting in a pew, why are you in church? *Salvation* will not jump on you. You have to accept Yeshua fully and completely without falsehood and pretense.

Anything that is worthwhile in this world you have to work at it. The same thought process applies to knowing Jesus, except for the love of God; this is **free**, and through His Grace and Mercy we are saved. I said FREE! Salvation costs nothing, but your time and falling on your knees - to accept the most precious gift that you will ever get in this life and that is Messiah Yeshua.

There is an Afro-American hymn Let us Break Bread Together that says; "When I fall on my knees with my face to the rising sun, Oh, Lord have mercy on me." These words represent a pure heart that is willing to accept our Holy God and His Son Yeshua who oozes with love. Seek God with all of your heart and know that He hears all of your prayers and concerns on this earth.

Yeshua is a loving and caring God, but He will not stand for the foolish of heart. If you continue down a spiraling path of evil, you will meet Him one day, but not as you think in Heaven, but you will be descended to Hell with your true father who is Satan. Repent and love Messiah Yeshua with all of your mind and soul, so you can obtain the life of *salvation*, be with your Lord and Savior for eternity. Saints of God let's get off the fence and get with Messiah Yeshua, time is ticking and the world is getting more immoral by the second. The "catching-away" is literally seconds away. It is no longer one minute before midnight it is one second before your time is up. Yeshua is knocking at the door!

Stages of Life

"During those days people will seek death but will not find it; they will long to die, but death will elude them." (Rev 9:6, NIV)

What is propelling Man to run from God in these Last Days? This is one question that has puzzled me for some time. I know that God is not puzzled by this question because He knows all answers to everything on this earth. The Lord God Almighty has given us the Wisdom to search and seek answers to all questions of life. This can be a life journey for everyone; we will not know all answers until we are in Heaven with the Father. One thought has come to me from Almighty God is that our Spiritual Leaders or Pastors are not teaching the Word of God as they should to their congregations. They are more concerned with keeping member- ship than teaching "End Times" prophecy that all congregations are yearning to be familiar with, in these "Last Days on Earth." Many will be left on earth and if they are ignorant of what is coming, then their last chance to enter into the kingdom of God will be nullified if they have no knowledge of Tribulation events.

I must give credit to Messianic Rabbis and some Pastors who

are not concerned about membership numbers but about saving Souls, they are teaching congregates to be ready for the great "gathering up" of the Saints. Scripture does say that Pastors will be judged more severely than lay people because they were called to preach and teach the <u>entire Word of God</u>, not just the parts they are comfortable with, but all books of the Bible. (James 3:1) We will search the Scriptures and seek some of the answers to the question of mankind running from God.

Jonah ran away from God when he was told to go to Nineveh and preach against the city because its wickedness had come up to God (Jon 1:1, 10, NIV).

King Saul ran away from God in the Spirit – when he decided to burn an offering to the Lord at Mikmash. King Saul sinned by burning an offering to God and let Satan crouch in his heart, thereby not asking God what he should do, before he marched out to war. This blatant act of disobedience led to Saul's fits of schizophrenia, as his kingship was "torn" from him by Jehovah. He developed an aggressive rage of discontent that caused him to chase David all over the Kingdom (1 Sam 13:1-15, TLV).

Prophet Elijah ran after Jezebel announced she would kill him for killing her prophets (1Kgs 18:46-19:9, TLV).

However, the ultimate runner was Adam after he and Eve had eaten from the Tree of Knowledge of Good and Evil. Adam made his sin worst by acknowledging that he was naked and hid from God with Eve (Gen 3, TLV).

So what does running from God have to do with death? [1]"In Hebrew, the word for *truth* is emet (אֱמֶת). When we remove the letter Aleph from the word emet you are left with the word "dead" (i.e., met: מֵת). The letter Aleph is the ineffable letter that represents oneness and preeminent glory of God. Therefore, if we attempt to ignore or suppress God in our understanding of truth, we end up with death. And since Yeshua told us, "I am the way (הַדֶּרֶךְ), the truth (הָאֱמֶת), and the life (הַחַיִּים); no one comes to the Father apart from me" (Jhn 14:6), those who deny His reality are in a state of spiritual death.

We simply cannot know the meaning of life apart from knowing the person Messiah Yeshua and His Glory. Mankind has been seeking the truth of God for centuries and yet men run, when confronted with reality and the <u>Real</u> truth of God. Consequently, disobedience and death to the Soul and Spirit occur by this act of denial, which brings about guilt, depression, self-denial, conflict, anger, sin, and faithlessness. The Scripture refers to death like the sting from the locust's scorpion that is so agonizing that people will seek death but death will fly away. Man is not allowed to die, and the agony from the pain lasted for five months (Rev 9: TLV).

This is truly a mystery. God will not allow man to die. Mankind will have to suffer the pain and anguish of sin for choosing to deny God Almighty as our Father. The Scripture clearly states that "Anyone who rejects His instruction does not reject a human being but God, the very God who gives you his Holy Spirit" - (1Thess 4:8, NIV). This is why the Word says to "resist the devil, and he will flee from you (Jas 4:7, NIV)."

It is far better to run from God than to do all of the things that God requires this is a mankind mindset. Mankind seems to think that if he can classify his life struggles to the earthly things of this world, then everything will be all right. Just looking around every day at the behavior of mankind is enough to cause one to be nauseous. We reject human life and self-respect of others. We proceed as if there is no God, the venom that proceeds out of individual's mouths is so appalling even the Angels in Heaven have turned their backs, covered their ears and eyes. So you know God has turned his back on individuals and nations (Ps 28.4, NIV). "Repay them for their deeds and for their evil work; repay them for what their hands have done and brought back on them what they deserve."

Have we completely consumed our Souls with possessions of this corrupt earth so much that we are damned to Hell? The quick answer is No. There is hope. Although very few people will admit that they are not consumed by possessions. Believe it or not, Christians will be the first ones that will speak up and say. "We don't have to have the belongings of this earth, and we can give them up."

Jehovah is in the business of testing all Souls to see if you are worthy to be a part of His Kingdom. He will break you, and you will have to either adapt or stay on the sinful course. The Majority of folks in the world don't know Yeshua, and they serve other gods, rather than the Creator of Heaven and Earth because He is nowhere in their psyche. All nations on earth believe their religion is the correct one. Various religions surround the earth and folks bow down to false wooden idols; that they can see, rather than the invisible Holy Almighty God.

So how would you surmise which religion is the correct one? This answer is easy. Let's first look at the obvious, Elohim said in Isaiah 45:18, NIV *"For thus says the Lord, Who created the heavens, Who is God, Who formed the earth and made it, Who has established it: "I AM the Lord, and there is no other."*

Another Scripture that comes to mind is Psalm 86:8-10 "He alone is God. There is none like Him among the gods. All nations should worship Him, the earth and everything on it." Elohim is the Creator; just gaze at the earth, the animals from the smallest to the largest. There is a God who is in the Heavens, who made this vast magnificent universe for us to live in, even the scientist now believe there is a God. "All the earth should fear the Lord and stand in awe of Him because He commanded and it stood fast. The heavens were made by His word (Ps 33:6-9, NIV)." Who wakes you up from your slumber every day, and gives you the breath of life in your body? If it is not God then who is it or what is it? If you don't wake up then, you are dead. God is a Spirit with millions of eyes and He is like nothing that you could ever imagine. We are given a hint of His glory and power throughout the Scriptures.

Let me say this, Satan and his minions are scared to death of God. They bow and cry out in anguish when they come in His presence. One example from the Scripture is from the book of Mark 5:1-20, (NIV), where a man is possessed by legion of demons. He was so tormented that he was naked in the graveyard in the region of the Gerasenes. Whenever he was chained with iron, he would break the chains. "When he saw Jesus, he ran and fell on his knees in front of him. He shouted at the top of his voice, "What do you want with me, Jesus Son of the Most High God? In God's name don't torture me!" For Jesus said to him, "come out of this man, you impure spirit!" No one has ever come back from the dead and said; "I now believe in God" because there is a great gulf separating the evil from the righteous Saints who have gone from this earth.

A television program aired in 2016 and again in 2017, it purported to give mankind choices on who is the god? I became so exasperated with the program that I turned to another station. The program centered on a man who went around trying to finding god and he would ask a folk of various religions who they thought God was and how do they worship God their god. Notice I am putting the word *god* in lower case because the gods of the television program were idols. I thought how many people were swayed in their belief of these idols, and proceeded to get caught up with this blatant idol worship?

None of the interviewed people mentioned Adonai or Yeshua. Almighty God was quietly dismissed like He did not exist. The Catholic Church was idolized as the ideal religion and thus praying to "an unknown god" was the main theme. My heart sank, and I prayed to Messiah Yeshua, please don't let any of your own people get dragged into this blatant LIE of Satan. We must be alert at all times and pray without ceasing (constantly) in order to overcome the deceitfulness of this wicked world.

The first stage of Life is learning about Jesus (Yeshua), repent of your sins, and give your life to Him completely. The second stage is developing the skills that the Holy Spirit has planted in our Spirit and let it grow by reading the Holy Scriptures daily, and connecting with others in the church and participating in church activities such as Bible study. The third stage is most important. Spreading the Word of God to others who need to know Jesus is essential. Not just to your family but outside of your social group. Social media is a good way to spread the message to all of your friends and co-workers who are mobile internet-based followers such as; Facebook, Twitter, Instagram, Blogs, Snapchat, Pinterest, and other public forms of media.

Joining volunteer groups in your community is another way to spread the message and even on the corners of your city with the "Corner Ministries." The Great Commission was given by Jesus to go to all the world and spread the message. Our Spirit must be pure, and our aim is to bring salvation. We cannot let life get us off the track. Satan is always scheming to get us to forget our purpose on earth.

We are not here to satisfy our wants and agenda, but to do the work and will of Jesus (Yeshua). We have to stay connected through prayer every day before we get started on our day. Make time in your schedule to pray every day as well as pray for your food. Not with just empty repetition of prayer, but a heartfelt prayer that will reach Heaven. How do we expect to get through this life without prayer? One can get through life, but the heartaches and pain will be so insurmountable that many want to end their life quickly with suicide. A legacy of Christian people will be important in these "End Times" so let's get back to basics; Almighty God is the answer, not the consumables of life.

God's Body is Outside of the City

"Therefore, to make the people holy through His own blood, Yeshua also suffered outside the gate." (Hebrew 13:12, TLV)

Jesus body symbolically is outside of the city in this verse because the sacrifice on the cross was outside of the city walls of Jerusalem. What occurred was un-holy, in this manner, He was humbled and emptied himself for us to be crucified, descended into Hades (hell) and broke through the enclosure of the gates of death. The gates of death had never been broken before and Messiah Yeshua rose up from the dead and ascended with a multitude to His Father. In Matt 27:52-53, (TLV) states "and the tombs were opened, and; many bodies of the Kedoshim (saints) who were sleeping were raised to life. And coming forth out of the tombs after His resurrection, they went into the holy city and appeared too many."

Messiah Yeshua had been scorned, mocked, beaten, and suffered for all of mankind's sins. Messiah Yeshua also suffered the grief of temptation by Satan during His forty day excursion to the wilderness. Everyone has experienced a wilderness moment, where we are thirsty and poor in Spirit, and only Almighty God can help us through the weariness in our bodies and mind. The wilderness experience is a test for the soul and spirit to become strong and mighty even in weakness. God said you were strong when you are weak. You must be strong in the face of sickness, death, loss of a job, family, and suicidal thoughts that may have permeated from the devil and his minions to your mind. When mankind looks to Messiah Yeshua on the cross, they see every sin; that will ever be committed in the entire universe until the end of time. [1]"Crucifixion was an ancient execution method, in which the criminal's hands and feet were bound or nailed to a wooden, cross-like structure. It was a capital punishment reserved for slaves, traitors," heretics", and usually the worst of criminals. It became widespread during the reign of Alexander The Great, but it still remains in occasional use in some countries." Even in our modern day people are crucified.

Messiah Yeshua is the Lord God of Heaven and Earth and His blood was shed for mankind outside the gate known as the Tabernacle symbolically, this was to fulfill the Scriptures written about Messiah Yeshua in ancient times. He loves His children so much that He wants them to come back to Him, only by our own self-will not by coercing. Sin crept into the garden; the spiral descent of man to the grave of death came suddenly. The very second Eve ate the fruit and gave it to Adam; eyes were immediately opened too good and evil. This is why Adam immediately lied to Jehovah Elohim about what he had done and why he was hiding. God cannot be mocked. He is omniscience and whatever man does Jehovah knows about it and He sees us. "In the middle to the throne and around it were four living creatures, full of eyes in front and behind (Rev 4:6, TLV)."

He will come back and get His, children, at the end of this age which is now called the "End Times." Messiah Yeshua promised, "for thou wilt not leave my soul in hell; neither wilt thou suffer thine Holy One to see corruption (Ps 16:10, KJV)."

Time is very short and Jesus loves His Creation and He is waiting for many to ask for forgiveness and to come to Him before it is too late. The judgment will commence, books will be opened and Jesus Christ will judge the wicked ones left on earth that did not obey and pretended to love Him. The wicked was found deficient having hearts consumed with evil intent. The time is up and they that are left are doomed to the fiery pit of Hell, there is no turning back. Jesus's heart will ache for their lost souls, but they made the choice to go to Satan and not to their Creator. Mankind let the multitude of lies spoken by Satan cover their hearts, they did not listen to the still small voice of Jesus speaking in their hearts.

Let me be clear to all who read the ordinances of Jehovah Elohim. Jehovah Elohim is not a vengeful God, but a loving God who made everything and allowed mankind to use the earth for his pleasure, and the earth is on loan to man. However, mankind will have to be punished for sins, and the punishment will be the ten plagues of Moses, but the plagues will be horrific in execution. Thus, your very Body, Soul, and Spirit are on loan to you, and you must keep it spotless, obey, love, and reverence Yeshua HaMashiach our Creator. Mankind has not honored Father God and what He created for mankind to enjoy. Father God will take back the earth and create a sinless universe where the ones who loved Him will live in peace with Jesus and His Father.

Once the timetable has started, and the Saints have been taken away, there are only seven years left for mankind to make changes in his life and come to Jesus Christ/Messiah Yeshua. Once the tribulation is over the time for redemption will be over, and very few souls will come to know Messiah Yeshua who was bound by Satan. There will be one thousand years of peace on earth whereby, all living souls that came through the Tribulation will live together in harmony on earth. Notwithstanding some wickedness on earth will appear, but it will be restrained quickly by

Messiah Yeshua because Satan will be bound in the abyss for a thousand years. Thus begin a new life in Jerusalem with King Messiah Yeshua ruling on earth in harmony with mankind.

Satan will be bound with a chain and put into the abyss. The Anti-Christ, false prophet, fallen angels, and demons will be put into the lake of fire burning with sulfur <u>alive</u> to be tormented. Satan will be set free for a short time after the one thousand years, to fulfill the words of the Bible in Revelation 20:10; to tempt the new Saints of the world after the one thousand years has passed. Keep in mind the people on the earth during the one thousand years will not know of Satan, but will be tested, once Satan is released from prison. Satan will go out to deceive the nations for his grand finale. Satan will be so fierce with his wrath that none can stand under this wickedness because he wants to be god and praised and honored. The imprisonment left him neutralized with a vengeance against God's Creation. Some of the mankind will be born to disobedience, against Jesus's laws and statues. Those who have not believed in Jesus (Yeshua) during the Millennium will die in their sin and eventually they will see justice for their unbelief. But swift destruction will be brought upon Satan and his angels. They will be thrown into the fiery pit of Hell forever, because this is the final battle by Satan at Megiddo, Israel. As compensation man will live with Messiah Yeshua on earth for all of eternity in the New Jerusalem. Get ready for an invigorating life with Messiah Yeshua a journey that will never end.

Chapter 3

Repentance

Fire in Man!

"AND THE TONGUE IS A FLAME OF FIRE. IT IS A WHOLE world of wickedness, corrupting your entire body. It can set your whole life on fire, for it is set on fire by hell itself." (James 3:6, NLT)

WHEN ONE THINKS OF FIRE, you think of the physical property of a blazing fierily gas that burns very hot and if you see blue that is the hottest part of the fire. So how does fire in a man come about? This is one of the questions I will dwell on doing our journey into what is Fire in Man.

Why does Man return to the earth as ashes which are the final stage before dust? Why does the pastor repeat the phrase "ashes to ashes and dust to dust" at a funeral? Adam was made from adamah meaning earth, or land in the Hebrew translation. Genesis 3:19, (NIV) states, "By the sweat of your brow you will eat your food until you return to the ground since from it you were taken; for dust you are and to dust you will return." Also, Ecclesiastes 12:7, (TLV) says, "Then the dust returns to the ground it came from, and the spirit returns to God who gave it."

Were we ever "fire" in our flesh, before we became flesh? The answer to this question is "yes", in a spiritual perspective we are born out of a *fire*. Almighty God our Creator is a flaming consuming fire. Elohim breathed His breath of fire into Adams' lungs, and the cold clay body became "hot" with blood, and Adam began to breathe the breath of Life through his body. This proves that we are made "hot" in a spiritual sense from *fire* known as (esh – אש) in the Hebrew language.

Our blood runs "hot" in our bodies and when we die, we are cold because the breath of fire has left the body. The breath of fire is the Spirit and the Soul of the person that has returned to Almighty God, who is the Creator. We are told to keep our sinful emotions and desires away from evil intent. The flesh lacks the capacity to evoke restraint unless we are connected to our Spirit because the flesh is part of the Soul. The Soul feeds on sinful thoughts that turn into regrets transmitted by demonic parasites from Satan. Fire burns hot according to dictionary descriptions, and it is fiery and very hot to the touch. It will burn or scorch the skin or completely consume a fleshly body. This is why as Christians we must be careful what we say with our "tongues" and what we do with our "bodies", they can be a blessing or a curse.

With our mouths, we can praise God Almighty, or we can expound profanities from our mouths. The same with the body, if there is sexual prostitution with our bodies then we have sinned against the body. For the body belongs to God, now He cannot be a part of an unholy union that is full of sin. If we are not careful, we can destroy our lives with lies, deceit, and sexual immorality. This is why the Scriptures explicitly say, "Be careful what you say and protect your life. A careless talker destroys himself (Prov 13:3, GNT)."

The Bible gives a great story about three Hebrew men who did walk in a fire. Scripture revealed, "I see four men loosed and walking about in the midst of the fire without harm . . . (Dan 3:25, NIV). The scripture references the Hebrew men who were put in the furnace by Nebuchadnezzar when they did not bow and worship his idol. The three men were Shadrach (Hananiah), Meshach (Mishael) and Abednego (Azariah) who came out of the fire unscathed without the smell of smoke. The fourth man was the Most High God's Son Messiah Yeshua.

This was not the first time man was put into a fire for testing. Abram (Abraham) was put into a fiery furnace by Nimrod for three days and only the ropes on his hands were burned off. Nimrod was trying to kill Abram because of his denial of idols in the land and his convictions of the Omnipresent Adonai laws. El Shaddai gave Abram grace and mercy because he was a pious man and followed the statues of God. After Abram's encounter with Nimrod - Abram left Ur of Haran and went to the land of Canaan.

The fire represents purification and devotion to God. Everyone must be ready to be tested, during your life for Messiah Yeshua, at any cost - even unto death if necessary. If you do die for God, you might be "absent from the body but present with Yeshua" for all of eternity. "[1]Fire represents mesirut nefesh which means, "self-sacrifice" in Hebrew. Should we not sacrifice our lives daily to Jesus? He is our Creator and He died for our horrendous sins because He loved us so much. Messiah Yeshua laid down His earthly body as the slaughtered lamb and went through the fire; which is the total devotion to Adonai His father for our sake. Without this, self-sacrifice, we would be doomed to Hell and never to come before the face of Adonai.

Our sin in the Garden of Eden was the most dreadful act of disobedience that has ever been recorded and executed in all of eternity. "[2]Since we know that Messiah Yeshua was "at the beginning with God" and is Himself God (John 1:1-2), the "Head of the House of Creation", He is none other than Yeshua the Mashiach (the Messiah) (Hebrew 3:4). This is further confirmed by the verse from Genesis 1:1 alongside the verse from John 1:1."

Why does Man return to the earth as ashes which are the final stage before dust? Ecclesiastes 12:7 clearly states, what occurs when you die; "Then the dust returns to the ground it came from, and the spirit returns to God who gave it." The gift of the Holy Spirit will breathe fire into us when we repent and acknowledge that Yeshua HaMashiach is Elohim, and at that moment we will receive the transformed heart of salvation. The moment you give your life to Yeshua then the Holy Spirit will reside inside of you, which is the (esh) – "fire" of Adonai.

God is our source of light spoken about in the scriptures as fire; you have to come before Almighty God, you must be transformed with the indwelling Holy Spirit who comes to reside inside true believers. He reveals Himself to us through our actions and attitudes. Jesus sent the Holy Spirit to us so that we could continue to gather more believers, before His return to "gather" or "rapture" us to the Bema Judgment (the Judgment Seat of God – 2 Cor 5:9-10) before the Tribulation. This is the judgment that all men must go through whether you are good or useless in God's Kingdom.

The Holy Spirit is the third Trinity of God, who is also made of fire and lives in the Spirit form inside of believing Christians. In Acts 2:3-4, (NIV) gives the best account of how the Holy Spirit rested on the Disciples in the Upper Room, "They saw what seemed to be tongues of fire that separated and came to rest on each of them. All of them were filled with the Holy Spirit and began to speak in other tongues as the Spirit enabled them."

Tongues mean other languages so that the visiting Jewish men from other countries could understand the meaning of this miraculous anointing, that Jesus (Yeshua) was arisen and was now sitting at the right hand of God, just as He had promised before he was raptured back to Heaven. Know God before it is too late and you give an account of your sins by <u>repenting</u> to Yeshua, for the hour of repentance is indeed at hand and you could miss Heaven and fall into the flaming fire of Hell.

Fire on the Mountain

"Then Elisha prayed and said, "O LORD, I pray, open his eyes that he may see." And the LORD opened the servant's eyes and he saw; and behold, the mountain was full of horses and chariots of fire all around Elisha". (2 Kings 6:17- NIV)

Prayer is a powerful force. Prostrating ourselves before Jehovah is the best way to get positive results from Him. Once we allow our Spirit to bend toward the acceptable journey to know Yeshua - then we will start to live according, to the scripture, that said; "you are not far from the Kingdom of God" (Mk 12:34).

We are consumed with our "get it now" version of prayer. We rarely really wait for a response from Messiah Yeshua; hence, a prayer that is looming in our hearts is never fully answered by God. I am included in this scenario. What I have found is, we can all have the correct solution to our prayers if we just are still and quiet before Almighty God. Being still is so easily stated, but very difficult to accomplish in our mortal bodies. This is a practice that takes time, prayer, silence, and consistent yearning to accomplish.

We have too many distractions and in-fighting with our Spirit to do or think about life's chaos. Being quiet and listening to the Holy Spirit speak to us takes time and tenacity, which we all have none? And yes, the excuses come forth like a wave of water - "we have to do this and that" neglecting the ultimate goal which is silence. Consequently, arriving once again back at square one with all of the sorrow, frustrations, disappointments, abandonment, discouragement, unfulfilled goals, and heartache.

What did Elisha really do that make him stand-out as a prophet? He had a simple prayer that went to the core of the problem. No flowery words or calling down of fire and brimstone. He simply asks God to "open his eyes that he may see." This is so simple. But there is more to this simple request. There was faith, trust, <u>repentance</u>, and a relationship with God that made the impossible, possible.

Why is it that the supernatural is so unbelievable to man? The intellectual man must have a scientific or logical answer before authentic belief can be manifested, and even then man's quest for knowledge is flogged with theorems, that is flawed and in most cases cannot be proven as fact or fiction. God cannot be explained from a test tube or from a fact that a research scientist has discovered or found from some experiment or archeological dig. God has always been and will be forever.

To truly understand God, you have to be still and have a conversation as simple as a child's prayer. So what are you speaking of you might ask? Until you decide to be still, and that means turning off all electronics and finding a quiet spot to clear your mind, then you will not hear from God. The simplest way to find Him is just asking God; "who are you", "how can I find you" and He will answer? not like you expected, so get ready for an unexpected answer.

You might want to try a prayer like the following:

"If you are out there God, please tell me who you are and where to find you? I am starving in my Soul and Spirit and need to be

refreshed with the water that you said is free to everyone - I believe you are out there God, so please come into my heart and forgive me of all of my sins. I believe in your son Messiah Yeshua (Jesus) and I believe He was born of a virgin, was crucified, died was buried and arose on the third day, and now seated at the right-hand of you Almighty God".

Even if you think you don't sin, you must believe and acknowledge Jehovah's Son Messiah Jesus (Yeshua). Jesus came and was born of a virgin, crucified, died and was buried, but arose on the third day and is seated at the right hand of Jehovah Elohim. You must wait quietly and see if you hear in your Spirit a still small voice say. "I heard you, and I forgive you and let's get going on your salvation journey." Don't be surprised when Messiah Yeshua calls you by name it might scare you at first, but know that He has answered your earnest prayer.

Of course, it may not happen just like I have purported but it will be close. God will even call you by name, or call, you His child and He will show you things that will prove He is really God. Whatever God says will be scriptural take note, and go to the Bible and confirm what you hear. Even if you don't own a Bible go to the Internet and type in the words you heard and you find a scripture.

Be forewarned, Satan is **very crafty** and he will be lurking around to distract and deceive you. He will mislead mankind into thinking he heard a voice that was from God. However, the voice is from Satan. He will distort the "truth" so be alert and aware of your surroundings and thoughts.

Satan can even come as an Angel of Light and has fooled many young Christians and seasoned Christians as well. If you don't know the story of Adam and Eve find a Bible and read Genesis 1-3, become aware that it is evil on earth and how mankind ended up in this predicament of sorrow.

The story of Elijah's replacement was Elisha whom God said

would take up the mantle for Elijah. Elisha believed fervently in Adonai because he had seen the miracles that God had performed through Elijah before he was taken up into the heavens. The cloak that fell back to earth that Elijah had worn while he was on earth, did not inherit a special essence from Elijah. When Elisha touched the river with the cloak, the waters parted. What made the waters' part? It was the prayer of Elisha to have doubled the portion of Elijah if he saw Elijah leave the earth – this is what made his fervent prayer possible.

Elisha spoke to God saying "Where is Adonai the God of Elijah" (2 Kings 2:14, TLV? before striking the water with the cloak. He also had to see Elijah leave in the chariot in order to get double the portion of the Holy Spirit from Elijah. "The fervent prayer of a righteous man avails much" according to Scripture. (James 5:16) Almighty God granted Elisha his prayer request because he was a righteous man.

Now the simple request from Elijah to God to reveal what was in the alternate universe known as the Third Heaven which is real, made the servant realize that God Almighty had deployed Angels of fire and Horses to fight the battle for man. If we would only take the time to worship God deeper and ask Him to reveal His will - we would be better off. The fire within God is consuming and moving all of the time in a spiral motion like the galaxies - "the glory of the LORD looked like a consuming fire on top of the mountain (Ex 24:17, NIV)."

The Israelites were very afraid when Moses went up on Mount Sinai, but Moses was not afraid, because he had been in the presence of Jehovah Elohim at the burning bush and knew that El Shaddai would not hurt him. Elisha had learned the same lesson as Moses to be humble with a repentant heart, and then he could go before God.

Little children have the purest hearts in the world before they are taught evil. Yeshua said, "anyone who does not receive the kingdom of God like a child will never enter into it" (Lk18:17). You have to be sweet, innocent, loving, no malice, or hate, forgiving, and willing to learn humility which is a childlike attitude.

We all fall short of being truly like a child, but we can ask to learn how to be good and pure in Spirit and Mind (Soul). These traits can be learned but you have to go through the fire, a testing period to prove you are really Yeshua's child. You can fail many times, but you will be able to take the test over and over again until you get it. Eventually, you will get the point, and you will have your mountain-top fire moment where you pass the test and ready to move to the next level in your life lessons.

What was the fire on the mountain? It was Messiah Yeshua's miraculous way of showing His obedient servant Elisha and the attendant that He will surround them with help if asked to assist. This wonderful God, who is Messiah Yeshua, displayed His love to the frightened servant; even though the enemy surrounded Elisha. They were protected on all sides by the *fire*, the fire represents the Holy fire of the Shekinah glory of Jehovah Elohim, which is the purity that cleanses and refines. The armies of Aram were not aware of the Shekinah glory that was surrounding Elisha and his servant from the wrath of Satan.

Now the King of Aram was at war with Israel and Elisha had been warning the King of Israel not to travel to certain places and to be on guard for the King of Aram. When King Aram heard that Elisha had been warning the King of Israel about his wicked tactics this enraged the King of Aram and he sought to cut off the head of Elisha and rid him from the earth. The LORD stopped the evil plan and sent a host of angels and horses to protect Elisha. Once they arrived in Dothan this is where the plot was foiled.

Now Dothan to Samaria was about 10 to 12 miles as Samaria was the Capitol of Israel at that time around 726-722 B.C.E. Now the attendant of the man of God (Elisha) arose early in the morning and behold he saw horses and chariots surrounding the city. He became afraid and told Elisha. Elisha told his attendant to not fear "for those who are with us are more than those who are with them." Then God opened the eyes of the attendant, and he saw the mountain was full of horses and chariots of fire all around Elisha (2Kgs 6:16-17, TLV)."

Elisha told the army to follow him after they had been struck with blindness and the King of Aram army walked right into Samaria and was captured by the Israeli army, and then they were promptly returned to their territory and the King of Aram. Consequently, he stopped raiding Israel's territory. As told in the scriptures, Elisha prayed to the LORD, "Strike this army with blindness." So HE struck them with blindness, as Elisha had asked. Elisha told them, "This is not the road and this is not the city. Follow me, and I will lead you to the man you are looking for." And he led them to Samaria.

We have many mountains to cross over or go through depending on your faith. Fire on the mountain with horses and chariots of fire with angels is a "Hallelujah" (הללויה) moment.

The Blue Flame and the Rainbow

"Things no eye has seen and no ear has heard that have not entered the heart of mankind – these things God has prepared for those who love Him." (1 Corinthians 1:9 (TVL)

Have you ever seen a blue flame with a halo around it? I saw eight lights one afternoon that was surrounded by a brilliant white light in the sky that was encircled with a blue flame. The flame had a magnificent rainbow-like halo that circled the entire white light. I could not stop thinking about the Shekinah glory of God on His throne, and how the throne must dazzle with His glory, as I gazed at the lights. The sun was hitting the eight lights just right and they produced the most dazzling sight I have ever seen. I blinked twice and the marvelous site quickly disappeared once the clouds covered the sun and the impressive site was gone forever but my recollection of this site was life-changing. It reminded me that God was awesome, and we really don't give Him the Honor and Glory, He deserves as our Creator and Father. It was truly an "Ah" moment of stunning beauty beyond this universe.

God had positioned me at the right moment to view this eye-catching wonder. Such humbleness, to experience the vast wonders of Adonai is enough to make you bow, before a Holy and Righteous God. If you don't believe in Adonai, this incident requires a person to stop; ponder the amazement and wonder of the site, and say "there has to be more to this earth." There must be a Triune God in the vast universe.

Isaiah encountered the marvelous Heavenly sight of Adonai in His temple and his explanation of the sight was more than mankind could ever envision or understand. "In the year that King Uzziah died, I saw the Lord, high and exalted, seated on a throne and the train of his robe filled the temple." (Isaiah 6:1, NIV). John's teleport to Heaven was depicted more fully "The One seated there looked like jasper and carnelian, and a rainbow gleaming like an emerald encircled the throne Revelation 4:3, NIV."

The Jasper stone is clear like a diamond where the carnelian is red like fire. Revelation 21:11 says that the jasper stone "shone with the glory of God, and its brilliance was like that of a very precious jewel, like jasper, clear as crystal." This is what I saw, the brilliance that was bedazzling; it brought tears to my eyes. What is my point? First of all most of us has never seen the clouds open and see a vision so clear coming out of the sky as the prophets of old experienced. Second, we have been shown so many times in the Word of God that He is real and His Son Jesus (Yeshua) came as a baby, suffered and died a horrific death for us this is proven by the Jewish prophets.

Yeshua was resurrected from the grave and this feat was proved by Messiah Yeshua's disciples (Talmidim in Hebrew) that he arose with thousands of new converts known today as Christians. *Who would follow someone and give their life to someone who did not arise from the grave, in addition, they saw, touched, ate and were pastored to by Messiah Yeshua for forty days before he ascended into heaven, to sit at the right hand of God?* Why did

Messiah Yeshua stay around? The disciples had to learn how to open their spirit and soulful eyes to the impossible and give credence to the ministry they were on embarking upon, while Messiah Yeshua was still appeared to thousands as proof of His resurrection. There had to be physical proof of the arisen Messiah for the Messianic Jewish Disciples to go forth and spread the "Good News." People had to visualize the risen Messiah and have a real relationship with Him in the flesh so that their ministry would have credence. A well-defined New Covenant was established with the newly anointed Christians, and it would give them the confidence to evangelize to all of the nations.

Messiah Yeshua promised a helper and this helper would never leave or forsake them. This third part of the Triune God is the Holy Spirit (Ruach Ha-Kodesh). The Holy Spirit is blue in color, and how do I know this because God has shown me this in a vision? The blue-white color of a flame is the hottest part of the fire and the "Blue color means (Heavenly Comforter: Holy Spirit)".[1] One might ask; why is there so much fire from Adonai? "Fire at Sinai, fire in Jerusalem, fire on the heads of God's chosen people:

- Fire is the root אש (eish) of Man איש (Iysh), breathed into the earth to create humanity.
- Fire is a reminder of the eternal nature of the human soul.
- Fire consumes that which is dead and transforms it into the light.
- Fire warms the righteousness and burns the wicked.
- Fire is a living symbol of resurrection." [2]

Romans 10:4 states that "For Christ is the end of the law [it leads to Him, and its purpose is fulfilled in Him], for [granting] righteousness to everyone who believes [in Him as Savior] Romans 10, (AMP)."

The fire that comes from the Holy Spirit is so "hot" that man cannot imagine the magnitude of His being. "The Holy Spirit stands on Jehovah Elohim's left-side and the blue flame that comes from Him is so powerful and hot that earthly Man has no way to determine the heat that is emitted from the flame. Just know the flame is blue and whiter than anything known to mankind. "The Holy Spirit only reveals His true self to those who really want to know the Triune God. The Holy Spirit is a Spirit and remembers every key point." Always acknowledge the Holy Spirit (Ruach HaKodesh in Hebrew) and thank Him for giving Knowledge and Wisdom. He is part of Jehovah Elohim because He is the third part of the Trinity. I know the concept of the Trinity; three in One can be confusing for Man, but this model is straightforward.

Where are the wise and powerful people? They cannot speak of things of God only to the flesh. The spiritual man has knowledge of wisdom, but the foolish man has no desire for knowledge and wisdom. Messiah Yeshua knows the spiritual things and all universal occurrences since He is Jehovah Elohim. Scripture clearly proclaims Yeshua's wisdom. "Yeshua puts a stumbling block to the Jewish people and foolishness to Gentile people (1 Cor 1:22, TLV)." For the message of the cross is foolishness to those who are perishing, but to us who are being saved, it is the power of God (1 Cor 1:18)."

We are in a perplexed state of denial in this 21 Century. Mankind that God made has fallen away from His statutes and commandments. Idol worship has become the flavor of the day and no regard to worship Adonai the Creator, but only to worship self-satisfaction. Mankind has gone a full circle; we are now living the days of Noah except this time, incineration by *fire* will be our demise. "They became filled with all unrighteousness, wickedness, greed, evil. They are full of envy, murder, strife, deceit, malice. They are gossips (Rom 1:29, TVL)."

Unfortunately, the world has become a junkie for technological devices. We are consumed with hand-held devices that have made us unresponsive to anyone or anything. We are like AI (Artificial Intelligence) robots that are controlled by our devices. It is a shame to sit-down at dinner, concerts, sports events, and social events, to see people pull out their cell phones and browse their Facebook, Instagram, Email, Messenger, Texting, Twitter, Snapchat, and Pinterest accounts; with no regard to engage in conversation with folks around them.

Even if they pretend to talk, they are not concentrating on you, but on the information, the device is giving them. How have we arrived at this reality? We are human beings, and we should connect in conversation with each other, not with a thing that has no spirit or soul. Did God give us a brain to use, and did He not want us to have a relationship with Him? How can you have a relationship with God, if all of your attention and concern is with a thing that is called a Beast? You cannot connect to Adonai via an electronic device. This is what the Bible warned us about. The Beast will be a talking thing that will control our minds. Revelation 13:15, (NLT) – "He was then permitted to give life to this statue so that it could speak. Then the statue of the beast commanded that anyone refusing to worship it must die."

We have been warned already by Elon Musk, the Tesla Chief not to trust the AI killer robots. He signed a letter to [3]"block use of lethal autonomous weapons to prevent third age of war robots. The technology for war machines will find man scrambling to control something that will take over man." The International Joint Conference on Artificial Intelligence (IJCAI) also sent a letter to the United Nations (UN) strongly urging them to stop the development of such heinous machines. The founders of the AI technology stated the following: [4]"Once developed, lethal autonomous weapons will permit armed conflict to be fought at a scale greater than ever, and at timescales faster than humans can comprehend. These can be weapons of terror, weapons that despots and terrorists use against innocent populations, and weapons hacked to behave in undesirable ways."

We do not have long to act. Once this Pandora's Box is opened, it will be hard to close." This is the spoken beast; it is here living in your home. What do you think the voice-controlled intelligent personal assistant services are that are being marketed to consumers? They are smart home devices connected to a cloud, to send data to a database, which updates and transmits all data to an unknown cloud on a multifaceted computer system.

Again the data is stored and these devices spy on you as well as your televisions, cell phones, iPad, laptops, etc. anything with a computer chip and a camera can spy on you and transmit data. We are being spied on 24/7, and we don't know it. Cameras are everywhere all over the globe, you can look at people anywhere and see what they are doing. There is nothing wrong with technology. I really like it, but we are now into overload and Satan has set up his final deceitful world power, for mankind, and he is using technology against us.

What has God really prepared for those who truly love Him? Just look around you and thank God for everything that you have for starters. You did not make yourself or did your parents make you without the hand of God by putting the seed into your mother and the miraculous body that was given to our first parents. God formed man from the mud of the earth and breathed fire of His breath into our lungs; thereby, mankind became a living soul. Who would do this, but a loving God? Only someone who really cares for you would go to all of the trouble to create you.

How can you not love someone who is nothing but Pure LOVE? A love that warms your inner being without asking for anything back in return except to love Him. An extraordinary life is waiting for you. It is a life not without trials or temptations on earth but, a life whereby, you can immerse your very spirit and soul into Adonai.

You can receive a trillion more blessings, mercy, and grace than you could ever imagine. The blue flame is the essence of whom Adonai is in this world and beyond into eternity. Our Father is light, and a consuming fire and He were before the creation of the earth and has always been. According to the Hebrew 1:3, TLV; "This SON (Messiah Yeshua) is the radiance of HIS (ELOHIM) glory and the imprint of HIS being, upholding all things by HIS powerful word."

I remember, I could not understand the concept of God as a child and would constantly ask my Grandmother and Parents who made God? The answer was implicit, He has always been, and there is no beginning and no end to Him. In Job 36:26, TLV "Behold, our God is exalted beyond our knowledge! The number of His years is unsearchable." As you can imagine this was truly confusing, and I know it puzzled me for years as a child. Then I asked Messiah Yeshua one day for wisdom and understanding so that I could start to understand the Scriptures and the Scriptures came alive like I had never known them before.

I did not fathom everything until my early twenties after much study of various languages and biblical translations. My musical background helped me tremendously, to comprehend the complexity written in the Scriptures when key points were fundamentally left ambiguous. As I looked for holy wisdom and understanding; I began an intensive study of the language of Hebrew and had several wonderful Messianic Jewish friends lead me to rabbinic books of study to advance my knowledge.

I discovered that God is light that we see, and darkness that we cannot see with our natural eyes; but only with our spiritual eyes. He is the wind, water, earth, sky, the entire universe including us. This layer of Almighty God is so deep, that it would be confusing for me to explain all of it to the natural man. One would have to be connected to God through the Holy Spirit, have a deep relationship with God, in order to appreciate the true Shekinah glory and magnanimous awesomeness of Messiah Yeshua.

Since God made us, we are part of everything that has been created. This is why Revelation testifies that "He has many eyes", His Spirits are everywhere and He does not miss a thing. He is Omnipotent (full of power), Omnipresent (everywhere at the same time), Omniscience (knowledge of everything and sees everything). The emotions are strong when I think about Yeshua (Jesus) who put down His Deity to come to earth; in the form of a baby and endure the sickness, hatred, being scorned, disease, hurt, pain, depression, dejectedness, and abandonment that we as mankind experience daily.

In the book of Jude 1:18-19, (NIV) the writer details the "End Times" of the un-godly and what you should expect when he says "In the last times there will be scoffers who will follow their own ungodly desires." These are the people who divide you, who follow mere natural instincts and do not have the Spirit. Jude warns of false prophets and teachers and to prepare for the coming of Yeshua by watching our behavior and repenting of our sins.

The ungodly and wicked are mentioned in the Scriptures as - "These people are [habitual] murmurers, griping and complaining, following after their own desires [controlled by passion]; they arrogantly speak [pretending admiration and] flattering people to gain an advantage Jude1:16, (AMP)." We are warned many times to avoid people who are wicked before Messiah Yeshua comes; however, few heed the warning.

In 1Timothy 3:1-5, (AMP) says "But understand this concept in the last day's dangerous times [of great stress and trouble] will come [difficult days that will be hard to bear]. People will be lovers of self [narcissistic, self-focused], lovers of money [impelled by greed], boastful, arrogant, revilers, disobedient to parents, ungrateful, unholy and profane [and they will be.] unloving [devoid of natural human affection, calloused and inhumane], irreconcilable, malicious gossips, devoid of self-control [intemperate, immoral], brutal, haters of good, traitors, reckless, conceited, lovers of [sensual] pleasure rather than lovers of God, [holding to a form of [outward] Godliness (religion), although they have denied its power [for their conduct nullifies their claim of faith]. Avoid such people and keep far away from them."

We are encouraged to keep a clear mind in all things and withstand hardships and do the work proclaiming the "Good News" of Yeshua. (2 Timothy4:5) We are living the life spoken about in the scripture of 1 Timothy, this proclamation should give you alarm to straighten out your life and get ready for the return of Yeshua. The hearts of men should be yearning to seek Jehovah and be a beacon of light for the unsaved souls. *Salvation* and *repentance* should be the goal for all men on earth to seek the face of Yeshua HaMashiach. If you are not seeking the Messiah then, you are doomed. All of our earthly possessions will be burned up in the fire, as so many people have found out when their homes are burned.

What we have on earth is nothing but dirt and rock and we cannot see that there is more to life than objects of our affections which will tarnish and turn to stone quickly. Kindness and love of mankind are the only things that will last. On your epitaph, you would want people to remember you as "The person who saved Souls for Messiah Yeshua" this would be a fitting epitaph. Our reward will be eternal life with God the Father, God the Son and God the Holy Spirit and life with our loved ones, who were obedient and now live in Heaven awaiting our entrance into the kingdom, to a life free of sin. Our entire being will be complete, and we will be home finally. Just remember this worn-out earth is not our final destination. For those who seek the truth of God there is eternity and love, but those who seek wickedness and evil, there is a home of eternal unrest in Hell. Earth will be restored to its original beauty without the thorns and hard clay, but rich with flowers animals, birds, fish, and the universe as it was intended before the fall of mankind. Remember this scripture from 1 King 19:12 "After the earthquake a fire, but Adonai was not in the fire. After the fire, there was a soft whisper of a voice." We now should look forward to the blue "sea of glass" with fire surrounding the Throne of El Shaddai. A perfect sinless immortal man will live in harmony with the Heavenly Holy Angels, who live in Heaven with Almighty God, God the Son and God the Holy Spirit. A sinful wicked man has no knowledge of this Heavenly pristine beauty, because of all the sin that crouches in his heart. His demise will be fire, but in darkness away from the face of Adonai.

Is Not My Word like a Fire?

"Is not MY word like a fire?" says the LORD, "And like a hammer that breaks the rock in pieces?" (Jeremiah 23:29, NIV)

Words are powerful, and they can either destroy or heal a broken Soul. Did El Shaddai not say to heed HIS words and to live by HIS commandments and statues? If you don't concede to live by the Holy Words, then they can be like fire in your bones when you hear the true Word of God. "Therefore thus says Adonai Elohei-Tzva'ot: (Lord God Almighty) because you speak this word, behold, I will make My words in your mouth fire and this people wood - and it will devour them. (Jer 5:15, TLV)."

Adonai is saying we must speak "truth", or the rocks will cry out and speak the "truth" instead. In this passage, Adonai was speaking to Jeremiah the Prophet. Jeremiah was warning ethnic Israel to heed God's Word; to repent and stop worshiping idols or Adonai would destroy the nation. We are the only living, breathing, beings on earth that has the capacity to make prudent and or un-prudent decisions.

We are the only beings, with the breath of LIFE given to us by

Adonai through HIS breath of fire into our nostrils. Without this breath of life, there is no life in the body. The heart has to have blood pumping blood and water through its veins or we will die. The blood is the life of anything that is created by God.

The soldier at the cross that pierced the side of Jesus knew that the blood was the key to the life of a man. This is why the Roman soldier pierced Jesus's side to see if he was dead, which lead to the releasing of the blood and water from Jesus's body. The action of the Roman soldier was to complete the written word in the Scriptures about Messiah Yeshua.

The testament of Christ's crucifixion (blood) and water baptism by John the Baptist, verified Adonai Elohei-Tzva'ot (Lord God Almighty) accepted His son's atoning sacrifice for mankind. In 1 John 5:6 (NIV) declares, "This is the one who came by water and blood - Jesus Christ. He did not come by water only, but by water and blood. And it is the Spirit who testifies because the Spirit is the truth."

Warnings come from God and He has sent them since the beginning of time. The signs have appeared in the Scriptures, the Heavens, and on earth. Yet man has failed to see or even acknowledge Adonai for anything. The Jews learned a fatal lesson from HaShem (G-d) for failing to obey His commandments and statutes; they were stricken with so many plagues in their country that they finally bowed down in reverence to HaShem. These Old Testament books could be vital to our lives if we would study and learn the hardcore lessons that Adonai taught His chosen people.

All of the prophets warned the people, and yet the Hebrew people (this is what they were called in the Old Testament.) did not stop idol worship and they forgot their God. We as a modern nation have broken every commandant and statue ever written, and we are being put to the test as we receive the wrath of God. This wrath has been clearly described in Revelation, Daniel, Isaiah, Zechariah, Matthew, and other books of the Bible yet we continue to disobey our Heavenly Father (HaShem) who loves us, but He will only stand for so much sin to be put forth into His face.

"But did not My words and My statutes, which I commanded My servants the prophets, overtake your fathers? Then they repented and said As the LORD of hosts purposed to do to us in accordance with our ways and our deeds, so He has dealt with us. Zech 1:6, NIV)."

Can you imagine your child day after day disobeying you until you have had enough even after you told them to stop misbehaving they continue to ignore you? Eventually, your patience wears thin and discipline must be established. So it is with God. He will send fire from HIS mouth and consume the wickedness. We are witnessing such wrath right now on earth from God. He has warned us and we still are "playing Christian-ease games" this is my name for our actions. We have people who say they are Christians, yet they are spewing their venom with words and actions that have nothing to do with Messiah Yeshua at all. However, they will lay hands on people to pray and have no clue that Adonai will not hear the words of the wicked.

As I have mentioned before, God's eyes are everywhere, all of the time 24/7 and He sees and hears every spoken and unspoken word you say out loud or in your heart. You cannot pretend with God. He is Holy and Righteous. God is [1]Omnipotent which means He is all-powerful and has supreme power and has no limitations. Omniscience means God is all-knowing and Omnipresence means God is everywhere at the same time."

"Many will say to Me on that day, 'Lord, Lord, did we not prophesy in Your name and in Your name drive out demons and perform many miracles? Then I will tell them plainly, "I never knew you; depart from Me, you workers of lawlessness." Therefore everyone who hears these words of Mine and acts on them is like a wise man who built his house on the rock. Matt 7:22-24, NIV."

Clearly, the Bible characterization of Almighty God is terrifying and to see God's wrath displayed on the pages of the Bible makes me weak in my knees. I don't know about you, but I truly don't want God's wrath poured out on me.

One instance in the Bible really frightened me to my core. In the book of Numbers, Korah and his group of 250 men assembled against Moses and Aaron. They came against Moses because they wanted to be exalted in the Hebrew community. They claimed that Moses and Aaron had exalted themselves above the assembly of Adonai. As you can imagine this did not sit well with Adonai.

When Adonai gets ready to do something it is "quick and fast" and you will not have time to take a breath. When Moses heard the accusations, he fell on his face. He told the people that Adonai would reveal who is HIS, and who is Holy in the morning. He told Korah, a Levi and his followers to take censers and present them to Adonai in the morning. He told them, Adonai would choose the Holy one. Moses also sent word to Dathan and Abiram, sons of Eliab, but they would not come out of their tents and said to Moses's messenger, that they would not have him Lord over them. This was a grave mistake because the truly anointed of God is to be respected.

So the next day Korah and his band of wicked men and Aaron appeared at the Tent of Meeting to meet Adonai and they put fire on their censers. Moses said to Aaron move back away from these wicked men. "Adonai spoke to Moses and Aaron saying, *"Separate yourselves from among this assembly so that I may consume them at once!* Numbers 16:20, TLV."

Moses and Aaron fell on their faces and pleaded with God for the wicked assembly. Adonai spoke and said to Moses "move away from the dwelling of Korah, Dathan, and Abirma don't touch anything of theirs and move back. If you touch anything of theirs, you will be swept away with them."

"Moses said to the assembly, "By this, you shall know that the LORD has sent me to do all these deeds; for this is not my doing. And if these men die the death of all men or if they suffer the fate of all men, then the LORD has not sent me. "But if the LORD brings about an entirely new thing and the ground opens its mouth and swallows them up with all that is theirs, and they descend alive into Sheol, then you will understand that these men have spurned the LORD (Numbers 16:28-30, TLV)."

As you can imagine immediately, the ground opened up (sinkhole) and they and their families and all of their belongings were swept away alive and then the earth closed over them and they were gone down into Sheol. The whole assembly panicked and thought they would be swallowed up as well and grumbled more loudly. You would think they would have shut up. No, as soon as they started grumbling (which is a sin) Adonai spewed fire from the Tent of Meeting and consumed all 250 men offering incense. Remember these men were wicked and were part of the Korah rebellious gang. As you can see if you go against God you will pay a heavy price.

You have two options on earth. Obey, *repent* of your sins or receive the wrath of God. God's wrath is imminent not come immediately, but it will come and you will wish you had not rebelled against the Creator. There are two choices in life with the Almighty God. Heaven or Hell (Sheol) and Hellfire will be the default if you make NO choice! Just remember this fact. Even if you make a choice, *you can still end up in Hell*. You can pretend to know God and pretend to be a Christian in church and not know Almighty God at all.

I was once familiar with a Christian pretender who joined the congregation, was baptized a year later was more of the devil than ever and denounced God. I had a pastor tell me that because, he knew the theology of the Bible, that did not mean he was a Christian and followed the word. He did not know the word of God only the theology.

I was quite stunned too, say the least. I was under the impression, if you went to Seminary School and learned theology then you would be a child of God. Or at least had a calling on your life from God, I was sadly mistaken. You can preach on Sunday or Sabbath and not know God at all. You can go to church because this is expected of you and can pretend to pray and not believe in God. You can feed the poor and clothe the needy and do all the right things. If you, never REPENT of your sins and TRULY, believe in your heart Messiah Yeshua (Messiah Jesus) is King of Kings and Lord of Lords' then you will not enter into the kingdom of El Shaddai.

This scripture states the obvious "Once the master of the house gets up and shuts the door, you're standing outside and begin knocking on the door, saying, "Master, open up for us" "We ate and drank in Your company, and You taught in our streets." But He will say, "I tell you, I don't know where you come from. Get away from Me, all of you evildoers! (Lk 13:25, TLV)."

Chapter 4

Belief

Yeshua is the WORD

YIRMEYAHU(JEREMIAH) 33:2-3, COMPLETE JEWISH BIBLE (CBJ) " Thus says ADONAI the maker, ADONAI who formed [the universe] so as to keep directing it – ADONAI is HIS name; 'Call out to me, and I will answer you – I will tell you great things, hidden things of which you are unaware."

A WELL-ORCHESTRATED strategy to create mankind was intentional, so that man would be able to choose his fate. God knew Lucifer would make a ploy to turn creation against Him. Lucifer's pridefulness was no surprise to God. Adonai created Man so that He would have a relationship with His Creation. God's plan was established before mankind was created, He knew mankind would sin. Adonai's Word will never be void. Jehovah Elohim and Yeshua HaMashiach knew the consequences of Man's fall, and the Word who is known as the Son of God, Jesus, Yeshua, Messiah Yeshua, Prince of Peace, and many other Holy names stepped forward and provided a way out for the redemption of sin that man brought upon himself.

Yeshua knew an unleashing of Hellfire would be brought upon man. He also knew once man sinned, man would be thrown into darkness and the light that Adam originally had received would be gone forever. There had to be a remission of sin and a true belief in Adonai as Creator and Father, otherwise, all of mankind would be thrown into a place of fire and darkness that would never cease. Once Messiah Yeshua stepped forward to be our advocate, man's fate was sealed from Hellfire. This fact is very important to the non-believer. In addition, Hell or Sheol was not made for mankind, but for Satan and his wicked angels who rebelled against Jehovah Elohim.

God loved us so much that He cultivated the earth enough, so we could live on earth and enjoy the fruits of our hands. Adonai selected a man who was righteous and had a blood-line that would be pliable enough to learn the "written word" long before the universe was ever established. Father God also knew the commandments and statutes would be passed down to the next generations to come through Abraham. There is a scripture that says "Before I formed you in the womb, I knew you." Jeremiah 1:5, TLV and we were sanctified by God.

God created all men that would exist on earth - the *good* and the *wicked* when Adam and Eve were created. This is a mystery to the common man, however; the fervent Saints of God will read the Scriptures, learn from the Word and become wise with under-standing. A Scripture in Luke describes the coming of our Messiah Yeshua after times are fulfilled. "And Jerusalem will be trampled by the Gentiles until the times of the Gentiles are fulfilled." (Lk 21:24, TLV). Also in Romans 11:25, TLV says "For I do not want you, brothers and sisters, to be ignorant of this mystery – lest you be wise in your own eyes – that a partial hard-ening has come upon Israel until the fullness of the Gentiles has come in; and in this way all Israel will be saved, as it is written."

According to my understanding of the Holy Spirit, the "fullness of the Gentiles" also means, when the last Gentile has been saved then the Tribulation will occur. We do not know when this will be, so this is an unknown mystery to man. These Scriptures are very clear that the Jewish hearts are hardened on purpose as punishment for worshiping idols in ancient time. Daniel 8:13 - speaks of the 2,300 evening and mornings then the Jews will be vindicated. This is the Tribulation period that the Ethnic Jewish people have to endure once the two witnesses appear on earth. They will be told that Messiah Yeshua was the One they were looking for they will be vindicated, but also grieved in Spirit, because they missed Him when He was on earth. These Holy Words tell of belief in Adonai and His Son Messiah Yeshua who died for our malevolence sins.

There are folks throughout the world who believe they will return to earth after a short stint in Hell (purgatory – Greek word) once they cleanse their soul they will have the opportunity to enter eternity and they will get to go to Heaven. This is a fabricated falsehood permeated by and condoned by Lucifer, to keep mankind in bondage with lies that are non-scriptural. Lucifer wants to kill off as many of mankind as possible and have them in his domain. This domain of darkness and despair will be in Hell with Lucifer, in his fiery domain as the king, with his wicked angels. Disobedience and unbelief have become the norm in our current society. Very few individuals believe in Hell or the Bible anymore. [1]According to the latest Gallup poll of May 2017 the record shows few Americans believes the Bible is the literal word of God, a staggering 24% the lowest in Gallup's forty –year trend."

God's word indicated many would fall away and become cold to the word. It is no surprise to God. He was expecting the down-ward climb. This is why the road is narrow for the righteous and very spacious for the unrighteous. Civilization in its current expansion is not ready for what is coming. Everyone believes God is going to forgive those who are doing the "good deeds" without repentance in their heart. Consequently, this concept is incorrect, the problem is God is Holy and man cannot understand immoral exploits are wicked. We were born with a sin nature bent against God, so when the nature is not transformed into the righteousness of God, through education of the Most High God, then we fall short of the mark to enter into HIS presence.

It was not a mistake that the Garden of Eden was given for Man to enjoy. However, Elohim wanted to know if Man would serve the Triune God without HIS intervention? Would he use the Wisdom and Knowledge given by Elohim to lead a life of righteousness in the Garden of Eden? Again God knew man would fall and the tree of Knowledge of Good and Evil was a test to confirm man's contempt away from the laws of Almighty God once sin was committed. Without true commitment and a yearning in the Spirit, to be with God the test of obedience would be nullified. Once the sin failure happened, the true test to be obedient began. The Triune God never wanted mankind to be with Him just because He made him. He wanted the man to be with Him because he loved God and wanted to be with HIM no matter what.

The blood sacrifices and the temple building were to prepare man for a committed relationship and life with God. A true unmarred relationship with Almighty God was the original plan that could not be imitated on earth with Lucifer (Satan). The blood sacrifice and temple building were to be for the righteous people, God organized a perfect outline for the Jewish people to follow so that they would worship Elohim and not idols. The punishment bestowed upon the Chosen People (the ethnic Jewish Nation) was a test and warning to everyone that followed Satan and his crew. Following the unrighteous and worshiping other gods, who could never create anything was an abomination to Elohim and HIS entire Creation. Once the fall of civilization happened, everything had to follow suit until Jehovah sent His Son Messiah Jesus (Messiah Yeshua) to provide the ultimate sacrifice of death - for all humanity from the beginning of Adam until the last human is to be born on earth.

No one will ever know God entirely because God has hidden mysteries that are too numerous for our mortal mind to comprehend because He is Holy and we cannot go to Him with our unrepentant hearts unless we <u>believe</u> and <u>repent</u>. Father God has no beginning and no end. He has always been and will be for all of eternity.

We are experiencing chaos and distress worldwide at an alarming rate that has not climaxed but is accelerating at supersonic speed toward destruction. God's Creation was never supposed to fall into temptation and destruction, but it was to be an everlasting union with Jehovah Elohim. Subsequently, Elohim's Highest Angelic Angel had a flaw and it was detected in Lucifer; he found a way to vindicate his demise and hate of mankind and facilitated a lie knowing a crafty lie would lead to "temptation". Lucifer was not happy when the man was made and he was not bowing down to the new Creation. He wanted all power and he saw a weakness in man – <u>desire</u>, so Eve became his target which consequently led to a fall leading straight into the pit of Hell with him.

Lucifer was very proud that day when mankind fell. He thought he had won and would become the reigning king. Lucifer was so <u>wrong</u>. God knew Lucifer would become proud because once HE made him, it was apparent the beauty of his being would get the best of him. ADONAI saw the flaw of his pride, and HE knew Lucifer wanted to be over HIM and everything HE Created. God gave him too much power, and he took that power to a level of sin in his proud heart that leads to a rebellion to overthrow Heaven. He wanted to be God and have a part of the Kingdom of Heaven for himself. How foolish he was to think God did not know - he had an unrepentant heart that would lead him to doom forever.

Satan's downfall did greave Jehovah Elohim; He saw that Lucifer wanted more power and recognition than what was already given him. A place called Hell had already been created when Jehovah Elohim created the earth, so it was fitting that Lucifer would end up in this Hellfire. A life of abandonment, fire, brimstone, darkness, and punishment was now meant for Lucifer and his gang of wicked angels.

God spoke to me in the Spirit saying; *"I am telling you all of this so that you can write more about me, and let those who truly believe in me, know that I AM THAT I AM. I am the one who holds the keys to life and death and all I ever wanted from Man was a true pure loving and devoted Spirit to ME without strings. Obedience and love with a wanting in your Spirit Man to worship everything about ME."*. Messiah Jesus is the HaMashiach (Messiah) He holds the keys now because He came to be the Lamb of Righteousness for Mankind. He will not return to earth until Jehovah Elohim tells him to come back to earth, and when He returns it will be very quick and those who truly know ADONAI will be gathered to HIM, they will be removed from the earth; thereby not going through the terrible Tribulation sent by Adonai. In 1Thessalonians 5:9, TLV says, "For God did not destine us for wrath but for obtaining salvation through our Lord Yeshua the Messiah."

In ancient times there was a prophet who prophesized about the coming of Messiah Yeshua; he was known as [2]"St. Ephraim of Edessa, the Syrian. Edessa is a city in modern Turkey, near Antioch, which is now called Antakya. He was born in the city of Nisibis, Mesopotamia in 306 and died in 373 B.C." A manuscript was found in 373.B.C. 15 centuries before the 18th century John Darby & the Brethren whom all came up with the Rapture theory.

Ephriam the Syrian as he was called wrote the following after reading Matthew 24:42 and 1 Thessalonians 4:13-17, where the saints that sleep and those that are awake will be "caught-up" ("to snatch out or away" in the Greek. The word "caught-up" is from the Latin "rapere" - "snatch away" and today the word is known as the ("rapture") this word means in the Greek form [3]harpazó - properly, seize by force; snatch up, suddenly and decisively – like someone seizing bounty (spoil, a prize); to take by an open display of force (i.e. not covertly or secretly)." The scripture says; "Therefore stay alert; for you do not know what day your Lord is coming." [4]"But, the phrase that has caught people's attention is from Section 2, of Ephriam the Syrian and it reads – "For all the saints and elect of God are gathered, prior to the Tribulation that is to come, and are taken to the Lord lest they see the confusion that is to overwhelm the world because of our sins."

Now, I must give proper credit to; the late Grant Jeffery, because he is credited with rediscovering this statement in 1995 and recognizing its significance to Rapture teaching. "Grant Jeffrey found the statement in Paul J. Alexander, *The Byzantine Apocalyptic Tradition, by (Berkeley: University of California Press, 1985), 2.10. The late Alexander found the sermon in C. P. Caspari, ed. Briefe, Abhandlungen und Predigten aus den zwei letzten Jahrhunderten des kirchlichen Altertums und dem Anfang des Mittelaters, (Christiania, 1890), 208-20." 1.*"

Millions of people will be left to make a final choice who they will worship. God will send chaos and fury, unlike anything mankind has ever seen and will ever see again. For those who have lived and worshiped Satan and his angels' Hell and damnation await them for eternity. Many fence-sitting Christians and *nonbelievers* hearts will turn colder and will not worship God, they will gladly give their lives to Satan. Here is the problem - you have to be ready in body, mind, and spirit for Messiah Yeshua to come back. So many people are not ready and want to live on earth, waiting for God to give them a sign or time to perform His handiwork.

People have mistaken that God wants them to wait. The time is now because the Holy Spirit is moving throughout the earth to save souls now before the coming. Once righteous Saints are gone and this includes Messianic Jews, then a time of anguish will be so enormous that no one will be able to withstand the inferno, except those with evil intentions. Many unsuspecting humans do not *believe* in Satan, they think he is mystical and has nothing to do with what is occurring on earth. They are so mistaken your VERY BREATH you breath is by God's GRACE and MERCY. If it were not for God's Grace and Mercy no man would live because all have fallen short of the Kingdom of God (Rom 3:23).

God said "I AM GOD" and I control everything that occurs on the earth in the heavens and beyond. God will give wisdom and understanding to those who ask for these attributes. Mankind has an arrogance and pridefulness; he believes he is smarter than God and he acquired his wisdom from educational intuitions. How foolish it is not to think God is not controlling man's thoughts. God said, "Did I not bring a deceiving spirit to King Saul so that he ran around the country trying to kill David?" (1Sam 19:9) "Did I not bring another deceiving spirit to Nebuchadnezzar to take Israel into captivity because of idol worship and outrageous disobedience?" (Jer 43:10)

God gave Man a free-will. A mind to make choices for his life whether good or bad, he has the ability to think for himself and to make selections for his lifestyle." However, Man is spirit and the spirit that God gave man prompts him to do good or evil. This is the choice that the Tree of Knowledge of Good and Evil presents to all of mankind. Your spirit will either prompt for good or evil. All men have God's Spirit and we know better than to sin, but the sin nature of the tree of Good and Evil will prompt you to do evil. This is where the choice comes in. You either want to do *right* or want to do *wrong*. You do get a strong prompting to do good but the Devil will send a deceiving spirit to prompt you to do wrong. After Satan presents a firm case to sin, you let the thought simmer in your mind, you rationalize to do wrong, and then you fall further into sin and unrighteousness.

Oh, my Brothers and Sisters. Don't you know God the Father, God the Son, and God the Holy Spirit loves you and Messiah Yeshua prays for us continually, that you will not fall into temptation, but we stray further from Jehovah daily and allow the worldly lusts to consume our bodies? We fight among ourselves because we want what someone else has or take what is not ours because we want it for ourselves. We kill because someone said something that you did not like. We kill children because they are in the way of our sinful lives. We act like dogs in the street because we think this is the only way to live. We change our status in life because we think this is the way to live, but Satan wants to destroy us, the sacred children of God Almighty, kill the Seed of Abraham for good. "How mistaken Satan is to think he can kill my righteous seed. There will always be a remnant left that is committed to God."

Do you not know God knew you before you were born?" Some people were to be with God and some were to be with Satan. All of this was "predetermined according to scripture." (Romans 8:29-30) Scripture states "some of you were wicked when you were conceived." (Psalm 58:3; Psalm; 51:5) "Some of you were righteous when you were conceived." (Jeremiah 1:50) The righteous group was to worship God and come to HIM, but some of mankind went over to the light of Darkness since they were tempted by the Devil and saw the bright light of the world. Many people thought this light was the real thing and fell so hard, that they could not come back, because of pride (Psalm 51:5.

Do you not know that God will take you back; all you have to do is repent, *believe*, and ask for forgiveness and He will take you back in a second? God said "As I stated before I did not create Hell and the lake of fire for my children. It was created for Satan and his angels" (Matthew 25:41). John 1:9-10, KJV says "If we confess our sins, He is faithful and just to forgive us our sins and to cleanse us from all unrighteousness. If we say that we have not sinned, we make Him a liar and His word is not in us."

Jehovah knew Satan would take one-third of the angels because Adonai wanted the angels to know they had a choice who they would worship, whether to follow Lucifer in his rebellion or stay with Almighty God and worship Him, whatever the choice - so be it. The fallen angels and Satan would have a life without light and the love of God; as a result, they chose fire, darkness, and damnation for eternity!

Belief can be described as having acceptance of something you cannot see until it takes place in the natural or invisible. This concept is complicated for an ordinary man, but the righteous man seeking God's heart understands the concept of *belief*. The reason the Jews had to sacrifice animals was to learn how to take instruction from HaShem (G-d). They had to learn how to get along as a community committed to HaShem, to love each other, and take care of each other in the process. The animal sacrifice was for the remission of sins for the entire community. However, they proceeded to mistake visible idols for what they could not see in the natural.

The ethnic Jewish community created a worship service that was conflicting with HaShem's laws, yet they were still going to the temple to bring sin offerings to HaShem which repulsed Him. This sinful nature we all have today, and we have forgotten about the Creator, hence we are led to doom and damnation if we don't *believe* and repent of our sins.

The Levitical process that Moses presented from HaShem to the ethnic Jewish people was a prototype on how to Worship HaShem as a corporate community and individually, which was preparing them for the "End Times" revival. "Hear, O people - all of you! Attention, O land and everything in it! Adonai Elohim will be a witness against you The Lord from His holy Temple (Micah 1:2, TLV)."

The Holy Temple existed before man and God's temple is where all of Creation will go and bow before the Most High God and give titles, offerings, praises, and blessings. The final temple is Jehovah Elohim who will be the temple, there will be no more "ark of the covenant", but the Light of Almighty God is the "ark" radiating from the Heavens. The Jews first then the Gentiles then all human life would know how to praise and love Jehovah without any promptings. This was the reason for the Holy Temple so Yeshua HaMashiach (Jesus the Messiah) could come down to earth and dwell with His creation and love them and they love Him and rule together on earth.

El Shaddai declares that: "My temple in Heaven is more glorious than Man could ever imagine. The earthly temple is only a foretaste of what my throne room and temple look like and all of the articles that are a part of my temple. However, again my Chosen People thought it best to pray and honor other Gods, and that not only angered Me but almost led to the destruction of all Men on earth. If it were not for the compassion of Noah and his obedience as well as Abraham, the promised seed of Abraham would have been destroyed." These are the words of Adonai that was given to me as I was writing this book.

All of the Heavens rejoiced when man was created and the Triune God was so overjoyed to have mankind who was called Adam was their firstborn who was full grown at the approximate age of 20 when he was created from the dust and dirt of the ground. The ground on which a man was created was sacred ground and his Spirit was pure and untainted without evil thoughts or images.

The Holy Spirit became the voice of reason and knowledge for

Man. Everything in Heaven is perfect, except for the one who had a flaw from the beginning and that was Lucifer. It seems odd that he was perfect, but there was a flaw that was not circular in him, he became the one Creation that was not perfect even though he was created perfect. If Jehovah Elohim had changed the events that were put in place, then the Angels would not have obeyed El Shaddai and all the Angels would have followed Lucifer. The flaw of evil that was placed in Lucifer was Jehovah's doing from the beginning.

The end of the earth will be quick and awful for Man, but the righteous will prevail. The new earth and the life of eternity will be the life you always envisioned but could never obtain. "I AM the Good Shepard and I will keep you from all evil and I will show you how to live life to the fullest." Declares the Lord!

Look at what is hidden in the word of God. Numerous mysteries exist that Mankind will never understand and it is deliberate. Not to confuse but to enable Man to see Adonai in all of His Glory and to know the true God of Heaven who is "I AM that I AM." In other words, "I will be what I will be" (or "I shall be") (Ex.3:14).

The Holy Spirit revealed to me the following: "My name is not known and no man knows my real name. Mankind should give up trying to say it. It is best to say Adonai as the ethnic Jewish people say or Jehovah or God (HaShem). My true name will be revealed to those who arrive in Heaven. The unknown name will be written on their foreheads Revelation 3:12, TLV "and on him, I will write the name of my God."

Mold Me and Mend Me

"Do not be conformed to this world, but be transformed by the renewing of your mind, so that you may discern what is will of God – what is good and acceptable and perfect." (Romans 12:2, TLV)

What does it mean to Mold Me and Mend Me?

God is trying to change the heart of the man, so we will have a heart that is mindful of Him, and concerned about the things that are godly rather than the things of the flesh. Jesus was on the earth for 33 years and for last three years of Christ's life He preached, taught, healed, and gave the secrets of how to live as a Christian (Gentile or Messianic) in a fallen world. Only the Gentiles and Messianic Jews embraced the message because they were hungry enough to be healed and saved by the man of God.

During the time Messiah Yeshua was on earth, ethnic Jewish people wanted to keep the laws that they were familiar with in their community. They did not want another prophet with flowery words, but they wanted a prophet to have a revolution on earth. Therefore, the Chosen people failed to embrace the true message of Messiah Yeshua. The One person they had been waiting for was thought to be a heretic rather than the true Messiah.

The disciples taught their Jewish brothers and sisters about the true Messiah, and Paul was commissioned by Messiah Yeshua to preach to the Gentiles. The irony of Paul preaching to the Gentiles was God's way of relocating His Word, from Jerusalem to the world. Even though the disciples went to other countries to preach, they did not have the same impact as Apostle Paul, since the disciples were commissioned to preach to their own ethnic Jewish people.

The disciples did not cover as much of the early ancient world in terms of spreading the Word of God as Apostle Paul. Nor did they establish as many churches for the Gentiles in foreign countries. There was a lot of disagreement as to the methods and theological interoperation of Messiah Yeshua's word, verses that the Tanakh taught especially with circumcision.

Apostle Paul, who had a name and heart change from Saul, became the catalyst for change for the small band of "The Way" (Christians) believers. The conversion from the murderer of Christians to a transformed heart for Messiah Yeshua is just remarkable. Paul's heart was *molded* and *mended* from his old Pharisee ways once his "eyes were opened" by the Holy Spirit - to a heart zealous for Yeshua. Messiah Yeshua was going to change Paul long before he met Stephen. The scripture says: "But when God, who set me apart from birth and called me through His grace, was pleased (Gal 1:15, TLV)."

Paul stood by and watched Stephen die from stoning, but he did not pick-up a rock to assist in the murder of Stephen. I believe he was already on his way to be converted; his heart was pliable and ready to be transformed. What made me come to this conclusion was Paul's visit with Gamaliel who was the Pharisee doctor of Jewish law. Paul questioned the sect of Christians known as "The Way" at that time and was on a mission to annihilate the new

Christians. Gamaliel gave him wise advice and said to "leave the men alone, if the Apostles are of human origin then they will fail. However, "if it is from God, you will not be able to stop them. You may even find yourselves fighting against God."(Acts 5:39, NIV) this was sound advice.

Today we have called Paul a Terrorist if he were killing Christians. The molding and mending became a quest for the Apostle Paul through the Holy Spirit's guidance. A devout law-abiding Jewish man, who was well trained in the Law of Moses, would be the one to carry the message to the Gentiles.

Jesus knew that Paul would be the one to bring salvation to the Gentiles; he was on a mission to kill all Christians who believed in the man-God who died on the cross. Paul went to great lengths to stop the disciples from spreading the Good News of Jesus Christ when he obtained the letter from the high priest.

"Meanwhile, Saul was still breathing out murderous threats against the Lord's disciples. He went to the high priest and asked him for letters to the synagogues in Damascus, so that if he found any there who belonged to "The Way", whether men or women, he might take them as prisoners to Jerusalem. As he neared Damascus on his journey, suddenly a light from heaven flashed around him. He fell to the ground and heard a voice say to him, "Saul, Saul, why do you persecute me? (Act 9:1-4, NIV)."

When Paul was on his way to Damascus, he met Messiah Yeshua. Interesting enough, Paul knew it was Messiah Yeshua. The vision of Adonai was so overwhelming that he lost his sight. I believe when Yeshua said I AM in response to Paul's question as to who was speaking to him, he fell on his face. For no man can see the face of Adonai and live according to scripture. I also believe Paul was so terrified by the vision that he was ready to be obedient to Yeshua HaMashiyach.

Paul was molded by Jesus to become His spokesperson to the Gentiles. The Gentiles would carry the message to the world for the Jewish people; who believed in the words of Jesus when He was on earth. The sects of Jewish believers in Yeshua today are called Messianic Jews or Jews for Jesus or just Yeshua believers. They have been around since Yeshua was on earth, but many of them were killed by their own people for their *belief*. Paul was ousted from the synagogue and Jews today consider him, not a Jew but a Jewish Hellenist [1]"devotion to or imitation of ancient Greek thought, customs or styles." In other words, they did not believe him and this is why the antagonist views were strong between Peter and Paul and the Jewish community. Paul had to obey Jesus after his encounter with the Lord on the way to Damascus if he had chosen not to obey only God knows what would have happened to Paul. Believe me, if Paul had disobeyed there would have been another person to carry the gospel. In Matthew 10:16, (NKJV) "Behold I send you out as sheep in the midst of wolves."

Jesus knew that there were scoffers and unbelievers and as a Christian, we are told to stand firm in our belief no matter what, because we are protected by God and the Holy Spirit. Jesus spoke to his disciples just before He ascended into Heaven giving them His final words of instructions. The disciples were to preach the Gospel and teach others to obey the statutes and laws of God to the entire world.

Prior to the great commission to go out and preach the word of Jesus to the world, Jesus had commanded the twelve disciples to go out and start preaching, healing, and driving out demons. "These twelve disciples of Jesus were sent out with the following instructions: "Do not go among the Gentiles or enter any town of the Samaritans. Go rather to the lost sheep of Israel. As you go, proclaim this message: 'The kingdom of heaven has come near (Matt 10: 5-7, NIV)."

Jesus gave a command to the twelve disciples early in His ministry to only go to the lost sheep of Israel. Proclaiming the kingdom of heaven has come near. This was to announce to all who had ears of understanding that the Messiah had come and to listen and obey, for God has sent the One the Jews had been looking for that was prophesied in the writing of the Tanakh. After the resurrection of Jesus from the grave and the suicide of Judas, then there were only eleven disciples left. The message now had been expanded to the small band of disciples. They now were given the message to go and preach to the entire world. Now some of them doubted Jesus after being with him for 3 ½ years still they did not have strong faith to *believe* Messiah Yeshua. It was not until the Holy Spirit came upon then at Pentecost, celebrated on the fiftieth day after the Jewish Passover that they because zealous to preach the Gospel.

I believe that some of the disciples would have been more effective, if they had not doubted, but had faith that was unshakable. If they had been more like Paul, who was firm in his belief; thereby allowing the Holy Spirit to lead them, rather than listening to their faithless hearts they would have been more effective in converting their own people. Paul persevered and suffered just like Messiah Yeshua, since he was the one that persecuted Yeshua the most after His resurrection.

The molding and mending of Paul are a good example of whom we should be in Christ, and our message to the world should be full of fierceness yet sweetness. We have to awaken our inner-selves and move beyond what we see and hear in the world and listen to the message of our heart from Jesus, who holds the key to our salvation and success on this corrupt earth. Many lessons can be obtained by reading the life of Apostle Paul and applying them to your life.

There were a rise and fall in the life of Apostle Paul. What do I mean by this? There was a low period of three days when Paul started his journey, after regaining his sight he established a *belief* that was on fire for Messiah Yeshua. The ministry did not take off for approximately seven to ten years; there he spent three years in Arabia where he was taught by Messiah Yeshua in the Spirit. He probably took the same journey that Moses took to Mt Horeb, where he could get closer to Messiah Yeshua and learn the teachings. This is my opinion. In 2 Corinthians 12:2 states, "I know a man in Christ who fourteen years ago was "caught up" to the third heaven. Whether it was in the body or out of the body I do not know – God knows." Apostle Paul is speaking about himself in the third person because the experience was so awesome that he could not express it any other way. Apostle Paul refers to his stay in Arabia in the following scripture. "I did not immediately consult with any human. I did not go up to Jerusalem to those who were emissaries before me, either. Instead, I went away to Arabia and returned again to Damascus. Then three years later, I went to Jerusalem to visit with Peter, and I stayed with him fifteen days. But I saw no other emissaries except Jacob, the Lord's brother (Gal 1:16-19, TLV)." Apostle Paul's demise came when he was imprisoned in Rome, but the message still went out even after his death. What a beautiful life when you can change a heart, that is full of darkness, to become full of life and light.

Harmony with God

"And He who searches the hearts knows the mind of the Ruach (breath of God, wind), because, He intercedes for the kedoshim (saints, the Holy ones) according to the will of God." (Romans 8:27, TLV)

Have you ever thought about a time where you were not in harmony with God's will? Many times we have all been bouncing around not listening and then when trouble arrives, all of a sudden you know how to pray and find God. The funny thing is God never left you, but you left God. Now what? God, where are you? So much anger and blaming the One, who truly loves you and the One who is not to blame. Satan is the one you should blame for the unharmonious relationship with God. The marvelous thing about God, He gives us all the rope we need to come back to Him. Often we hang ourselves, trying to find the answers and yet, just before we jump off the cliff of life, we are saved by Jesus through His grace and mercy. A "still small voice," that says, "I will never leave you nor forsake you."

Jesus speaks softly and says *"Child, what are you doing? Don't you know I am always here for you, and I never leave you? But you left me and now the disobedience is deep within your soul, and you think, I commanded this awful thing on you. I did not, but the lies of Satan became a reality in your Soul and off you went on your merry way toward destruction."*

How do you make a connection with God now that you are on the outside of God's favor? Swallow your *silly pride*. Get on your knees and pray and ask for forgiveness. This must be a genuine prayer of repentance, not the normal weak prayer. Your prayer should say; "I will not do this again." Then in a few days you have forgotten your repentance to God, forgot His Son Jesus, and you are already back to your normal sinful ways. A thoughtless prayer was prayed and, you forgot that you were not sincere in your efforts to believe.

Let me clue you in on a few things. God is not to be mocked! This is clearly stated in the Bible. You see friends; you really don't know the true Creator who is Almighty God. He is not only our Creator, Lord, Master, and Father, but He owns you. Jesus was also known as Yeshua in the Hebrew language died and was raised from the grave for you. Yeshua suffered so much for you, that there is no way in this life you could ever pay Him back for the life He has given you.

You cannot work your way to Heaven or into the life of Messiah Yeshua. Almighty God (El Shaddai) had to turn His head when His son was crucified on the cross. Jesus had never been separated from God even as a baby born on the earth. Jesus was still part of the Trinity with no separation. Now, because of sin brought on by our sins of disobedience; Jesus had to stand by himself for that last moment in time, away from His Father. God had to shed a tear, and then everything went meshuga (crazy).

There was a loud clamor of screams on Golgotha, then the earthquake and the rocks split into which borne the fierce winds that turned into a vortex of blackness, that was so deafening that the people screaming in the rain, ran away in horror of the sounds of the wind and rain. This was the agony of God having to turn away from His Son.

Then dark clouds gathered quickly over Jerusalem, the temple curtain was ripped in two from the top to the bottom the sky turned black like night and the sun refused to show her face. There was a total eclipse of the Sun. [1] The altar spoken of here is not the sacrificial altar. The messenger is offering incense, which is only offered on the incense altar (Exodus 30:1) that stood before the curtain which veiled the Holy of Holies.

This curtain was torn at the point of Messiah's death. It was torn from top to bottom as an action of a grieving Father tearing His garment. This action was the unveiling (Revelation) of the Holy of Holies and means that this altar is now seen immediately before the throne of HaShem in the heavens. Many saints that were dead from the beginning of time were resurrected from the dead and were walking and showing up at various places.

I am sure many people died that day, just from the mere sight of seeing people who were dead a few days before the crucifixion and now, walking around alive, this must have been frightening. God reconnected with His son after the three days and three nights which incidentally started on Wednesday afternoon and Messiah Yeshua arose on early Sunday morning known as the first day of the week. This is where the awesomeness of Jehovah Elohim is terrifying and loving all at the same time. Messiah Yeshua our Lord and Savior got up and brought with Him the saints of old into Paradise.

The very great stone was rolled away from the tomb by a mighty Angel and I am sure the soldiers fell dead from the light and fear of the awesomeness of the Angel, who opened the tomb and Yeshua the King of Kings walked out. No wonder the soldiers were killed and others lost their minds and still others were told to say the body was stolen by the Apostles. The scene at the tomb was something that could not be explained by our human eyes or mind.

How does this harmony with God correlate to the universe? Harmony in a musical context is "any simultaneous combination of tones or chords." The Triune Godhead made everything from a spoken Word thereby making all things musical. Why would I say this? Satan was the head musician in the Heavenly place. He wanted to be worshipped, and he lost his place in Heaven and was thrown down to earth and his final place is the pit of Hell. Music has order and form that is always changing and merging into glorious melodic melodies.

Music also has discord where melodies clash against the diminished tones and fugal interpolations, yet this entire disharmony is resolved before the composition is completed making the harmony magnificent. I can expound extensively about music with confidence because I have been a musician for years. Everything on earth has a purpose, and the earth is constantly moving and developing new lands and water masses just like a musical composition. However, just like a composition, there has to be a beginning and an ending.

The earth and the universe are coming to its end; this is why it moans and groans with earthquakes, and all kinds of storms. The vast universe is always creating new galaxies and constellations, even though there are black holes being found in the universe that is swallowing a large number of galaxies. All of this harmony is part of the greater scale of praise and worship that the universe magnifies toward Almighty God.

If the universe has harmony, then we were created with harmony as well to coexist with the Triune Godhead, but we lost our footing when sin appeared. Our harmony is the love of Jesus Christ who died to save us from further destruction and to have a relationship with Him and His Father. So we are a song without an ending with broken minor and diminished chords that cannot be resolved until we have a perfect relationship with our Creator.

The perfection of the musical composition will be complete from beginning to end when, we are with the Father in Heaven, and there will be no more crying or heart-ache. Our bodies will be whole, and we will have new songs to sing with a new Spirit that will be perfect, just like a perfect melodic melody. When Jesus calls us unto Himself, then the harmony will be complete. The song will resolve and make music that is so perfect, only Heaven will be able to sing the chordal structure with infused melodious instrumental melodies, that only God will give us. It will be so polyphonic with cluster chords the human ear will not be able to sustain the splendid sound that will be emitted from the musicians, who are in the Heavenly choir and orchestra. The voices of Heaven will reach notes unheard of in this realm, and the instrumentation will be unparalleled to anything, we as God's creation could ever create or imagine. This is true harmony with God. Oh, what joy, my heart is full of happiness with the thought of El Shaddai's magnificence.

There is another kind of harmony that is not part of God but against God. That is disobedience. When we don't obey then, our harmony with our Creator is disjunctive. "I appeal to you, dear brothers and sisters, by the authority of our Lord Jesus Christ, to live in harmony with each other. Let there be no divisions in the church. Rather, be of one mind, united in thought and purpose (1 Cor 1:10, NLT)."

Jesus warned us to get along with each other; otherwise, we fall into sin and disobedience. Harmony is especially critical in our churches. If we have division, then Satan has a stronghold and he will make sure to separate the church and then the harmony will no longer exist. Satan's main purpose in life is to make us sin. Don't forget Satan is the first one at the church on Sunday or Shabbat and the last one out as he is turning out the lights. Don't forget he is an angel of light that has fallen and can deceive anyone so you have to "Stay alert! Watch out for your great enemy, the devil. He prowls around like a roaring lion, looking for someone to devour (1 Pet 5:8, NLT)."

The Devil is good at putting wrong thoughts and ideas into our minds. The evil thoughts will not develop if we ask Messiah Yeshua to remove all unrighteousness from our minds. The trouble comes when we ponder the thought, then the evil thought pierces your mind (soul) and you are now in trouble because you are bound, by the devil and the harmony with God has been broken. This is why we have to ask for forgiveness daily because sometimes controlling the un-godly thoughts, can be difficult when we are with ungodly people in our workplace, family, friends, and alone at home.

"Keeping harmony can be very difficult," many people will say. I am not going to pretend that it is easy to be in harmony with Jesus 24/7, because I am always asking for forgiveness and seeking scriptures, to help me become the person that my Heavenly Father wants me to be. But I can prevent myself from sinning when I have a conscious awareness of Jesus all day in my mind. I can then ask for assistance from God, and then I am able to prevent sin from happening. Rev 17:17, (TLV) says, "For God has put it into their hearts to do His will, and to be of one mind, and to give their royal power to the beast until the words of God are fulfilled."

In Genesis 5:19-24 there was a man named Enoch. "And Enoch continually walked with God, and then he was not there because God took him. Gen 5:24, (TLV)." Enoch was a godly man who walked in harmony with God at 65 years of age. Once he had his son Methuselah who was his first born, he was taken by God. Meaning, he was walking and talking with Adonai one day and the next second he was in Heaven with Adonai. We don't know if Enoch walked with God prior to 65, but the meaning here is that he was faithful to God and walked and believed in

Almighty God. You would have to surmise that Enoch was righteous because God's eyes are everywhere 24/7 never sleeping, so HE knew the Spirit and Soul of this man (Gen 5:22, TLV).

The scripture states that he was translated meaning he was raptured to Heaven. Enoch was raptured for a short time then returned to teach his children the correct way to live according to Jehovah Elohim. This is the first recorded Rapture in the Bible. Why was he taken? Enoch did not question everything as we do today, he just obeyed God. [2]"His walk with God was by faith and not by rules and regulations. Enoch is the man who represents the church." This is the future coming of Jesus to remove (Rapture) His church from the earth because He did not intend for His church to go through the Great Tribulation. "Because you have obeyed my command to persevere, I will protect you from a great time of testing that will come upon the whole world to test those who belong to this world (Rev 3:10, NLT)."

So what does this have to do with harmony with God? Everything that is faithful and true to the Word of God has to be righteous in love and in harmony with God. "Here is my servant whom I chose, the One I love, in whom My soul takes delight; I will put my Ruach (Spirit) upon Him, and He shall proclaim justice to the nations (Matt 12:18, TLV)."

Jesus came to set the captives free (Luke 4:18) from bondage on this earth that was set up when our forefather and mother gave Satan to rule over us. Our harmony was broken when the fruit on the tree in the Garden of Eden was eaten. We sit in darkness until we connect with Jesus (Yeshua). We have to ask Jesus to forgive us of our sins and ask Him to come into our life because we believe He is the Son of God, who was born of a virgin, suffered under Pontius Pilate was crucified died and was buried and arose on the third day and sits at the right hand of the God Almighty, who is the Father of Messiah Yeshua.

What joy and adoration we can have when we are faithful,

peaceable, loving, believing, and true to Jesus Christ who gave everything for us so that we might one day be with Him in Paradise. All Praise is for the Lord! "Live in harmony with one another. Do not be proud, but associate with the lowly. Do not be wise in your own eyes! (Roman 12:16, TLV)."

Hallelujah! I Made it!

"Pray for the peace of Jerusalem - "May those who love you be at peace." (Psalm 122:6, TLV)

Whenever the final Word on earth is spoken then, God will call us home, then we can all sing "Hallelujah! I made it! We all must pray for peace on the land of Israel and the city of Jerusalem according to the scripture. If we do pray for peace, then we will prosper, but this must be from the heart if we really love the city of God. This is where our Spiritual roots lie at Mount Moriah where Abraham built an altar to Jehovah (the Lord will Provide.). God had given 120 years of grace to the world before He destroyed it by Flood. As time passed, the people did not repent and God's anger against mankind was so fierce, that He decided all life on earth would be destroyed due to the wickedness of man on earth. Noah found grace in the eyes of God and he and his family of eight individuals were spared the punishment. These pious souls were selected to replenish the earth.

We are now in the "Age of Grace" again according to the Bible, "as in the days of Noah it will come like a thief in the night (1

Thess 5:2)." In Luke 21:22, (TLV), God says, "For these are the days of punishment, to fulfill all that has been written."

We are living in the "Age of Grace" or some call it the "Church Age" because salvation can come to anyone who believes in the Son of God who is Messiah Jesus (Messiah Yeshua). It is very important that anyone who does not know Jesus will come to the knowledge of Him quickly for tomorrow is not promised to anyone. We do not know when Jesus will come back and once He does the "Age of Grace" will be over and you will not have a chance to find Messiah Yeshua.

Jesus never left us without a song or a Word of comfort, whereby we can speak and change the hearts of so many confused, doubtful, unbelieving, tormented, and stressful people. God will lift up all of those who go beyond the normal Sunday/Sabbath Christian life. We were left with a mission to go out and preach the Word of God and make sure everyone that will hear/listens to the words of Jesus would come to salvation.

This is our final time to get right with God for ourselves and bring the salvation Word of Yeshua to everyone. Not just to our family and friends, but in the streets to those on the corner, the homeless, the drug addict, the prostitutes, the vile wicked men and women of our time. Everyone will bow down one day to Adonai according to scripture "every knee will bow and every tongue will confess that Yeshua is Lord (Phil 2:11)."

Jesus is definitely coming back, sooner than most believe and it is important to bring as many people to the knowledge of Jesus as soon as possible. For Hell is not where we should be, that pit was not made for God's most precious Creation. We were made to rule over the earth with our Heavenly Father. If we do transform our heart and hear the "still quiet voice" of Jesus speaking to our Spirit, then we will be left on the earth, destined to burn forever in a fiery pit for all of eternity.

We want to be with our loved ones who know the Lord. The

Hallelujah is the praise that we have to give our Father. He is the One who gave His life for us. Why do we always do what we want rather than what Father Jesus wants? It is the sinfulness of our flesh, and the flesh always wants to be fed. We are disobedient because we have not removed enough of our flesh from our lives, to live the life that Jesus requires of us to live. We ask for forgiveness, but that is not enough when we know better.

We must commit our flesh to the Father and ask Jesus to help us to remove the sinfulness that keeps us from fulfilling the path of righteousness that is required for our full salvation as a Christian. Christianity is not just a word that means that you are a follower of Christ. It means you are a changed individual and you believe that Jesus is worthy of all praise and your body, mind, and spirit belong to the living Heavenly Father.

You have dedicated your heart to the life of righteousness; you have put away all idols from your life that can prevent you from seeing the true God. Idols can be anything that removes you from your loving Jesus, that allows you to bow down or standing up for something that is not holy. Just remember Nebuchadnezzar and the three Hebrew Men who were put in the fiery furnace. They refused to bow down to an idol of Gold made in the image of Nebuchadnezzar. Yeshua HaMashiach saved them because God's Commandments say.

"I am ADONAI your God, who brought you out of the land of Egypt, out of the house of bondage. "You shall have no other Gods before Me." Do not make yourself a graven image, or any likeness of anything that is in heaven above or on the earth below or in the water under the earth. Do not bow down to them; do not let anyone make you serve them. For I, ADONAI your God, I am a jealous God, bringing the iniquity of the fathers upon the children to the third and fourth generations of those who hate Me (Ex 20:2-5, TLV)."

You do not have to live in a life of utopia and mystical

thoughts; you have to pray for Jesus to lead your life and move your psychological thoughts to love of God and not of self or selflessness. You were bought with a price and that price was Jesus's life, and every knee will bow down and everyone will see Messiah Jesus when He returns and it will be so glorious and wonderful. The sky will flash with lighting and the Father of Heaven and Earth (HaShem in Hebrew) will come back as He left us on a cloud and everyone on this earth will see Him. This is your Hallelujah moment!

"It is written: "As surely as I live," says the Lord, "every knee will bow before me; every tongue will acknowledge God (Rom 14:11, NIV)."

"Then I heard every creature in heaven and on earth and under the earth and on the sea, and all that is in them, saying: "To the One seated on the throne and the Lamb be blessing and honor and glory and power forever and ever! (Rev 5:13, TLV)."

"After this, I heard what sounded like the roar of a great multitude in heaven shouting: "Hallelujah! Salvation and glory and power only belong to our God; Praise the Lord (Rev 19:1, NIV)."

Marvelous and wonderful thoughts zoom past in my Spirit when I just think about how an awe-inspiring God can make you want to stay in His presence always when you feel the love and safety that He brings just from His presence.

It took only a spoken word from God to make Abraham move away from his family and move to an unknown land. Abraham did not have the distractions that the modern world has, and he had an open Spirit to God because he saw the idol worship that was being performed by his family. Abraham was bound by his father's (Terah) polytheism and this lead Abraham to draw closer to his ancestor Shem. Terah was the chief officer or pastor to Nimrod (King Nimrod of Babylon) who built the Tower of Babel.

Now [1]"Abraham spent many years in the house of Noah and Shem and received instruction from them. Thus, he learned all the details about the Flood from the very men who built the Ark and survived the Flood. (Noah knew Methuselah for many hundreds of years, who in turn knew Adam for many hundreds of years, which means that Abraham received reliable information about everything that happened since the very first day of Creation!)." [2]" Abraham was the tenth generation removed from Noah, being a direct descendant of Shem, (Noah's son), the father of all the "Semitic" peoples. When Abraham was born, Shem was 390 years old, and his father Noah was 892 years old. Abraham was 58 years old when Noah died. Abraham was made welcome by old Noah and Shem, who taught him all they knew about God and the ways of God."

Abraham knew God intimately because of his relative's teachings and his own experience. When HaShem (God) spoke Abraham moved without question because He knew God would lead him. He did have moments of disobedience just like us today, when he went to Egypt and lied to the King and later listened to his wife, and had relations with Hagar to produce an offspring. The point I want to make - if Abraham could make it out of polytheism, then there is hope for all of us to make the change and become the God-fearing people we were meant to be. Make sure you follow the commandments that Jehovah Elohim has brought to us. Follow the nine gifts of the spirit and make sure you are a holy and righteous Christian who is zealous for Messiah Yeshua HaMashiach.

Summary

Whatever you believe or don't believe there will be mysterious things on this earth that will not be explained until the end of time. It is most important to remember the four points that have been discussed. Purification, Salvation, Repentance, and Belief in Jehovah Elohim and His Son Yeshua HaMashiach is most important for a successful and full life. Get ready for the most fabulous exit from this earth into a gleaming dimension that you could never imagine. We will march into the Kingdom of God and receive our crowns of gold. We will throw down those crowns to Almighty Father in worship and praise to the King of Kings and Lord of Lords. This harmonious event will be the culmination of a life on earth that was wretched with all kinds of sorrow.

The church service in Heaven will never end, because we will travel, sing, play instruments, create new inventions, learn Hebrew, have seminars with the Prophets and the Apostles just to name a few events. We will always have Jehovah Elohim as our Father and we will never want for anything ever again. We will be able to learn all there is to learn and just when a million years have passed, we will just be at the beginning of our learning capacity.

The New Jerusalem will be brought down to the renewed earth, and the earth will rejoice with all of Heaven for it will never groan again. We will be in our glory clothes; that we had when our forefather was created, however this time it will be washed by the blood of our advocate Holy Yeshua HaMashiach. Get your house in order so that when your time on earth is finished, you will be ready to enter Heaven and enjoy the greatest event in the universe, the presence of the Adonai Elohei-Tzva'ot: (Lord God Almighty). **Website and Blog**: http://drmozart18.com

Thank you for reading the book. If you enjoyed this book or found it useful in search of knowing Yeshua/Jesus, I'd be very grateful if you'd post a brief review on Amazon. Your support really makes a difference, and I read all the reviews personally to get your feedback and make this book even better. Thanks again for your post!

Books By Author

Just the Edge of God: The Touch of His Garment is All We Know

Take the journey from knowing Almighty God to seeking a meaningful relationship with Jehovah.

The publication provides real-life examples to ponder.

Scriptural verses to help bond a relationship with Jesus Christ.

More Scriptures and references for the curious individual.

For folks not committed to Christ and have questions regarding Jesus, the book motivates people to press on to the next level in their quest for truth.

Ardith Arnelle Price has mentored many people to change their lives and discover a genuine relationship with Jesus Christ. Her evangelist style of teaching and praying has helped people of all ages and demographics. Take the journey with her and find universal comfort inside your essence.

Looking Through the Sea of Glass: Four Inspirational Words from God to Live a Fulfilling Impactful Life

Have you ever recognized how difficult it can be to understand Scripture?

Ever investigated the depth of the sea near the shore and watched the inhabits swimming through rocks and coral?

If so, you are privileged to see the exposed depiction of a mirror of Father God's translucent magnificence divinity.

The book will cover four inspirational words from a Messianic and Christian viewpoint:

Purification

Salvation

Repentance

And belief in Jehovah Elohim and His Son Messiah Jesus

The book is a handbook for anyone searching to improve their walk with Messiah Jesus or find salvation. Looking through the Sea of Glass will create a yearning in your heart to learn and study the Holy Scriptures and be a "fired-up" Christian for Messiah Yeshua.

The Grave is licking its Lips

Apocalyptic End-Times Thriller. Noah and Michaela, successful professionals, acquired everything young millennials could ever crave as a lifestyle.

They had children, a house in the burbs, and worldly possessions. Then a flood invaded the city and dragged a hellish demon into their lives with fury.

The Narrow Door Blazes with Fire

An Epic Fantasy of End-Times. One evening, the small city of Marsh Harbor experienced an unusual occurrence that shook the friends from their homes.

Helen Smith, a bank Securities Manager and her neighbors Noah, Michaela, and her supervisor, Stephen Rana, battle demons. They discover a deep portal opening to the depths of Hell, demonic conflicts, and bloodshed.

Exalted Above All Gods, Son of Perdition and the Wrath of God and the Battle for Earth Series, 3

She wants to stay alive. But a sexy madman commands worship. A network bot triggers murder and death.

Arvvada, Colorado, a futurist town, is a chaotic pre-Millennium home of a band of doomsday computer engineer preppers. *Exalted Above All Gods,* inspiring story is where loyal humanoid astronauts and computer professionals spiraled into the Tribulation.

Becky Weinman, a persecuted Messianic Jew and engineer, plummets into the second half of the Tribulation with a charming, sexy villain who mandates total worship. A deadly computer bot exists on a space station computer mainframe, ready to detonate. Sabotage and deceit from Becky's engineering team members prompt an urgent inquiry from the humanoids, and murder ensues. A brief love confrontation turns fatal. An intense surprise riveting ending awaits the engineers.

* * *

Thank you for reading the book. If you enjoyed this book or found it useful in search of knowing Yeshua/Jesus, I'd be very grateful if you'd post a brief review on Amazon. Your support really makes a difference, and I read all the reviews personally to get your feedback and make this book even better. Thanks again for your post!

Website and Blog: http://drmozart18.com

About the Author

Michigan-based author Ardith Arnelle Price writes inspirational books and Christian Apocalypse Sci-fi thriller novels.

She has been a lifelong writer since fundamental school, creating supernatural worlds and characters.

Ardith Arnelle Price has received outstanding recognition for her book, *Looking Through the Sea of Glass*, from the 28th Annual Writer's Digest Self-Published Book Awards in 2020. In addition, *Just The Edge of God* climbed #78 in the Kindle Unlimited top 100 books in July 2021.

Ardith is an accomplished musician, educator, bible studies enthusiast, an avid golfer, information technology, web designer, and studies foreign languages.

She lives and works in Michigan with her husband. Ardith is a member of several civic and social organizations: Sigma Gamma Rho Sorority Inc., Sigma Alpha Iota Fraternity (Music), American Association of University Women, Civitan International, Rochester Writers, and Women in Publishing.

Published books: *Just the Edge of God, Looking Through the Sea of Glass, The Grave is Licking its Lips, The Narrow Door Blazes with Fire,* and *Exalted Above All Gods.*

Social Media:

Webpage & Blog: https://drmozart18.com/
LinkedIn: https://www.linkedin.com/feed/

Instagram: https://www.instagram.com/DrMozart18/
Twitter: http://www.twitter.com/@drmozart2
Facebook: https://facebook.com/ArdithPrice18
Amazon   Author   webpage: https://www.
amazon.com/~/e/B08CY65CFW

Appendix

Some of the Names of God and Hebrew Words Used in the Book

Adonai – Hebrew name for God. Both "*Adonai*" and "Elohim" Are Plural Hebrew Nouns "*Adonai*"

    Elohim – God in Hebrew

    El Shaddai – Almighty God in Hebrew

    House - temple

    Jehovah – *Jehovah* Ezer, the Lord our Helper

    Kohanim – priests in Hebrew

    Messiah – Anointed One

    Meshuga – Meshuga means crazy or foolish (Yiddish משגע meshuga from Hebrew məšugga

    Ruach HaKodesh – Holy Ghost in Hebrew

    Triune GOD - consisting of three in one (used especially with reference to the Trinity). The Triune Godhead. God the Father, God the Son, God the Holy Spirit.

    Yeshua – "Yeshua" in English Bibles; Ezra 2:2; Neh 7:7).

Yeshua, in turn, was a shortened form of the name Yehoshua ("Joshua" in English Bibles). Which means "*Yahweh* saves" (or "*Yahweh* is salvation").

Yeshua HaMashiach - Jesus, the Messiah

Bibliography

Amplified Bible, AMP, Biblehub.com@2004-2014 Biblos.com

BibleStudyTools.com, Love, Elwell, Walter A. "Entry for 'Love", "Evangelical Dictionary of Theology." 1997, Copyright©2014.

"Blood Moon and Jewish Destiny", by Rabbi Ari Enkin, http://unitedwithisrael.org/the-blood-moon-and-jewish-destiny/, April 13, 2014

Complete Jewish Bible, CJB, copyright© 2018 Bible Study Tools, Salem Media Group.

English Standard Version, ESV, Biblehub.com@2004-2014 Biblos.com

Good News Translation, GNT, Biblehub.com@2004-2014 Biblos.com

International Standard Version, ISV, Biblehub.com@2004-2014 Biblos.com

King James 2000 Bible, KJ2000, Biblehub.com@2004-2014 Biblos.com

New American Standard Bible, NASB, Biblehub.com@2004-2014 Biblos.com

New International Version, NIV, Biblehub.com@2004-2014 Biblos.com

New Living Translation, NLT, Biblehub.com@2004-2014 Biblos.com

Messianic Jewish Family Bible, Tree of Life Version, Messianic Jewish Family Bible Society, Syracuse, New York, United States of America, Copyright©2015

Oxford Dictionaries – online, @2014 Oxford University Press, oxforddictionaries.com

References

"Abraham's Early Life- Jewish History", Chabad.org is a division of the Chabad-Lubavitch Media Center, 2017. www.Chabad-Lubavitch Media Center Accessed October 10, 2017.

Bogmilsky, Moshe, *"Chabad.org, "Fire-Water-Wilderness"*, Ask the Rabbi-1993-2017, http://www.chabad.org/library/article_c-do/aid/2836571/jewish/Fire-Water-Wilderness.htm, Accessed October 17, 2017.

Brodkin, Jon, *"Google Releases Glass Source Code, Declares Platform Open to Hackers"* 4/29/2013, Ars Technica, website: https://arstechnica.com/information-technolo-gy/2013/04/google-releases-glass-source-code-declares-platform-open-to-hackers/, Accessed Nov 1, 2017.

Brown, Yaakov, Spiritual Leader of Beth Melekh Congregation, Auckland, and N.Z. *"Blog: Revelation8: Seven Shofrot (Lambs Horns)*, 7.18.2015, https://www.bethmelekh.com/yaakovs-commentary---15081497151214931513-1497150615111489/revelation-8-seven-shofrot-lambs-horns. Accessed on October 27, 2017. With permission.

"Ephraim and the Rapture ",Manuscript: *On the Last Times, the Anti-Christ, and the End of the World, A Sermon by Pseudo-Ephraem Section* 1", Jim McClarty and Grace Christian Assembly, http://salvationbygrace.org/current-qa/ephraim-and-the-rapture/, Accessed Oct 18, 2017.

Jeffrey, Grant R., _Heaven the Last Frontier_, (Bantam Books, 1990) pg. 59-60.

McGee, J. Vernon, *The Epistles, Hebrews* Chapter 8-13,pg 80, Thomas Nelson Publishers, 1991.

"Musk, Elon leads 116 experts calling for outright ban of killer robots", *Sunday, Guardian News and Media Limited* last modified. https://www.theguardian.com/technology/2017/aug/20/elon-musk-killer-robots-experts-outright-ban-lethal-autonomous-weapons-war. Accessed August 20, 2017.

Parsons, John J., "Covenant of Fire", Hebrew4Christians.com; Parashat Bereshit. hebrew4christians.com. Accessed October 17, 2017.

Strong's Greek translation -726- harpazó (ἁρπάζω)-properly, seize by force;snatch up, suddenly and decisively – like someone seizing bounty (spoil, a prize); to take by an open display of force (i.e. not covertly or secretly)." Strong's Greek Concordance, -online, © 2004 - 2017 by Bible Hub, Accessed Oct. 18, 2017.

Notes

2. Salvation

1. Online Dictionary.com – Salvation, accessed December 7, 2018. www.dictionary.com/browse/salvation

Stages of Life

1. "Hebrew Word of the Week, Emet- Truth", January 12, 2017. http://www.hebrew4christians.com/Glossary/Word_of_the_Week/Archived/Emet/emet.html

God's Body is Outside of the City

1. Jay Simon, 2010, Most Cruel Execution Methods", October 20, 2017. http://www.historyrundown.com/10-most-cruel-execution-methods-of-all-time, History Run Down 1

3. Repentance

1. Moshe Bogmilsky, "Chabad.org, "Fire-Water-Wilderness", Ask the Rabbi- 1993-2017, October 17, 2017. http://www.chabad.org/library/article_cdo/aid/2836571/jewish/Fire-Water-Wilderness.htm
2. John J. Parsons, "Covenant of Fire", Hebrew4Christians.com; Parashat Bereshit –; October 17, .2017. hebrew4christians.com

The Blue Flame and the Rainbow

1. Yaakov Ben Yehoshua (Jacob son of Joshua), Blog Genesis9: "A Covenant Sign) accessed August 28, 20. Bethmelekh.com
2. Yaakov Ben Yehoshua (Jacob son of Joshua), Blog "Shavuot: From Sinai to Moriah" accessed August 28, 2017. Bethmelekh.com
3. "Elon Musk leads 116 experts calling for outright ban of killer robots", *Sunday, Guardian News and Media Limited* last modified August 20, 2017.

https://www.theguardian.com/technology/2017/aug/20/elon-musk-killer-robots-experts-outright-ban-lethal-autonomous-weapons-war.

4. "Elon Musk leads 116 experts calling for outright ban of killer robots", https://www.theguardian.com/technology/2017/aug/20/elon-musk-killer-robots-experts-outright-ban-lethal-autonomous-weapons-war, Sunday, August 20, 2017, Guardian News and Media Limited or its affiliated companies, all rights reserved. October 20, 2017

Is Not My Word like a Fire?

1. Definition – "Omnipotent, Omniscient and Omnipresent God: Definition & Overview," accessed Oct 11, 2017. Study.com

4. Belief

1. ,"Record Few Americans Believe Bible is Literal Word of God", May 24, 2017 Gallup.com, Social Issues, May 15, 2017
2. "Ephraim and the Rapture ",Manuscript: On the Last Times, the Anti-Christ, and the End of the World, A Sermon by Pseudo-Ephraem Section 1,Jim McClarty and Grace Christian Assembly, http://salvationbygrace.org/current-qa/ephraim-and-the-rapture/,Oct 18, 2017.
3. Strong's Greek translation -726- harpázō (ἁρπάζω)-properly, seize by force;snatch up, suddenly and decisively – like someone seizing bounty (spoil, a prize); to take by an open display of force (i.e. not covertly or secretly)." Strong's Greek Concordance, -online, © 2004 - 2017 by Bible Hub, Oct. 18, 2017.
4. "Ephraim and the Rapture ",Manuscript: On the Last Times, the Anti-Christ, and the End of the World, A Sermon by Pseudo-Ephraem Section 1,Jim McClarty and Grace Christian Assembly, http://salvationbygrace.org/current-qa/ephraim-and-the-rapture/,Oct 18, 2017.

Mold Me and Mend Me

1. Merriman-Webster, Hellenism, online Dictionary, © 2015 Merriam-Webster, Incorporated

Harmony with God

1. Yaakov Brown, Spiritual Leader of Beth Melekh Congregation, Auckland, and N.Z. "Blog: Revelation 8: Seven Shofrot (Lambs Horns), 7.18.2015,

accessed on October 27, 2017. https://www.bethmelekh.com/yaakovs-commentary---15081497151214931513-1497150615111489/revelation-8-seven-shofrot-lambs-horns.
2. J. Vernon McGee, The Epistles, Hebrews Chapter 8-13,pg 80, Thomas Nelson Publishers, 1991.

Hallelujah! I Made it!

1. Website: Chabad.org is a division of the Chabad-Lubavitch Media Center, 2017, www.Chabad-Lubavitch Media Center, "Abraham's Early Life- Jewish History", October 10, 2017.
2. Website: Chabad.org is a division of the Chabad-Lubavitch Media Center, 2017, www.Chabad-Lubavitch Media Center, "Abraham's Early Life – Jewish History", October 10, 2017.

Made in United States
North Haven, CT
13 February 2024

48690663R00085